"THE CRYSTAL RIVER PICTORIAL"

CASEIN PAINTING BY DELL A. MCCOY

"Action along Thompson Creek"

"THE CRYSTAL RIVER PICTORIAL"

By Dell McCoy and Russ Collman

Produced By
SUNDANCE LTD.
DENVER

A small Class 56 Denver & Rio Grande narrow gauge 2-8-0 engine passes the rock formations in Thompson Creek Canyon, pulling empties upgrade for the coal mines. The Aspen & Western Railway reportedly ran only one train of coal during it's short existence -- due to poor management -- and never purchased railroad equipment to further the venture.

CASEIN PAINTING BY DELL A. MCCOY

"THE CRYSTAL RIVER PICTORIAL"

By Dell A. McCoy and Russ G. Collman

Published by
SUNDANCE Limited / Denver

Dell A. McCoy, *President and General Manager*
Russ G. Collman, *Vice-President and Editor-in-Chief*
Peter E. Voorheis, *Executive Secretary*
David S. Digerness, *Consulting Editor*
Robert A. LeMassena, *Special Consultant*
Jackson C. Thode, *Special Consultant*

Prepared and Produced by
SUNDANCE Publications Division

Russ G. Collman, *Picture Editor*
Dell A. McCoy, *Art Editor*
Viva A. McCoy, *Manuscript Editor*
Karen Hoffman, *Editorial Assistant*
Chloris Nickelson, *Quality Control*
Peter E. Voorheis, *Chief Photo-Technician*
Tom Donner, *Color Reproduction Consultant*

Printing, Typograpyy and Binding

Dell A. McCoy, *Production Manager*
Joy Beauvais, *Production Assistant*

Typesetting by Mil-Man, Inc.
Binding by Dieter Bookbinding Company

Peter E. Voorheis, *Index*

Printed in the U.S.A. by SUNDANCE Limited
P. O. Box 6385, Denver, Colorado 80206

SECOND PRINTING
— 1973 —
International Std. Book Number
(ISBN) 0-913582-04-2

Cover Photograph hand-tinted by Dell A. McCoy.
From the collection of John W. Maxwell.
Photographed by Morrison A. Smith.

The scene shows Crystal River & San Juan Railroad locomotive Number 1 rolling downgrade with a mixed train, departing from Placita, Colorado, on November 11, 1941.

INSPIRATION — Carved in statuary Colorado-Yule marble at the studio of Lorado Taft in Chicago, Illinois, this work of art was produced by Kathleen Beverly Robinson, sculptor.

FOREWORD

The Crystal River Pictorial is the first detailed photographic record of the short-line railroads that once operated in the scenic Crystal River district of Colorado. Beyond this fact, however, *The Crystal River Pictorial* is much more than "just a railroad picture book." This vivid pictorial brings together, in one book, the largest and most representative selection of photographs ever printed - that portray the hauntingly beautiful, but remote, Crystal River region of the Rocky Mountains.

Here, for the first time, is the complete pictorial story of the fabulous Crystal River country -- that legendary mountain district high in the Elk Mountain Range of central Colorado. Encompassing an area of less than forty miles in length, the Crystal River district has a unique history to Colorado and the American West. While the "booms and busts" of most Western regions were based on silver and gold, the pioneer economy of the Crystal River country was primarily dependent on rich deposits of coal and marble. This unusual combination of mineral deposits brought about the development of equally unusual industries to tap these treasure hoards.

Included in this rare scene was some of the most unusual railroading ever conducted in Colorado -- a state renowned for its mountain railroads. Embracing both narrow gauge and standard gauge lines, as well as both steam and electric operations, these railroads created a high-

ly picturesque and vital part of the history of the Crystal River Valley.

Until publication of *The Crystal River Pictorial*, there had never been a comprehensive photographic portrayal of the little railroads of this region -- and there had never been an adequate guide to show where these railroads operated. This volume fills these unknown gaps.

The Crystal River Pictorial not only takes you back into the boom period of the district, but it also shows you what the region looks like today -- in modern full-color photographs. Besides this graphic presentation, the book presents detailed maps of the railroads of the valley prepared through the use of aerial photographs provided by the U. S. Geological Survey.

During the early days of the Commercial era, promoters planned to run railroads to nearly every settlement in the district -- and over nearly every mountain pass. Even such places as Crystal City and McClures Pass were not beyond the realm of possibility for the land sharks and expediters of paper empires. Eventually all the gradiose schemes boiled down to what became a somewhat weed-overgrown set of rails meandering up the Valley of the Crystal from Carbondale to Marble -- with three improbable branches wandering off into the High Country above the river.

This "golden era" lasted for only too brief a period. By 1942, all of the rails

had been removed and the last two steam engines had been shoved onto a siding in Carbondale, awaiting their fate. Somehow, when the last locomotive chugged down the valley, it signaled the end of a grand age. Business attempts have continued since that time with uncertain amounts of success, however, the district will never be the same again.

In the beginning of the commercial era, men of high stature founded and directed the enterprises of the Crystal River district. Only when rich and corrupt outside interests began to worm their way into the activities of the valley did the "good times" begin to fade. Self-seeking union agitators and stock market manipulators did much to undermine the companies that employed most of the people in the district. Eventually this money-grubbing element caused the very economy of the Crystal River Valley to crumble into ruins.

Today's generation looks upward to the beautiful Elk Mountains, high above the Crystal River. Skiing, hiking, camping, fishing, hunting and "just plain relaxing" attract thousands to the region. Meanwhile the coal mines of the Coalbasin area once again are pouring forth valuable tonnages of "black diamonds." And perhaps in the not too distant future, the American building industry will once again utilize marble in the construction of the nation's houses of learning and governing, as well as for great cathedrals and monuments. It might even be that Americans someday will be able to find room

CONTINUED ON PAGE 6

FOREWORD continued

in their complex and materialistic society for beautiful marble works of art.

Or is it actually true that Americans can afford everything but beauty in their cities?

RUSS COLLMAN
DENVER -- 1972

In this Ektachrome, Treasury Mountain rises in the distance to 13,464-feet. This shot was taken off the road to Schofield Park, looking southwest. Walking through here, one can appreciate the greenery of the heavy undergrowth and the sweet smell of sparkling fresh water coming from a tumbling mountain stream.

PHOTO BY DELL A. McCOY

COLLECTION OF BILL SMITH

After coming down the Crystal River valley through a winter snowstorm, engine Number 1 of the Crystal River & San Juan Railroad couples onto cars in front of the depot at Carbondale, Colorado.

TABLE OF CONTENTS

LAY OF THE LAND

Panoramic Map of the Crystal River Railroad

Terminating at a point originally called Satank, near the present site of Carbondale, Colorado (elevation 6,000 ft.), the Crystal River flows into the Roaring Fork River, a tributary of the Colorado. At the opposite extreme, the Crystal River originates in the remote Snowmass Wilderness Area in the heart of the verdant Elk Mountains. The headwaters begin in Gunnison County — flowing first westward, then northward--tumbling on through Pitkin County and emerging onto a broad valley in Garfield County.

The Crystal River region of Colorado is considered by those who have viewed it as one of the most beautiful areas in the Rocky Mountains. The snowcapped Elk Mountain Range hovers over the valley to the east and south, while towering Mount Sopris -- at an elevation of 12,823 ft. -- stands guard at the north entrance of the valley. To the west, the rolling Huntsman Hills conceal vast coal reserves under their mantle of green.

CONTINUED ON PAGE 11

The color photo on the facing page shows one of the Denver & Rio Grande Western's unit trains heading out of Carbondale with 5,000-tons of Coalbasin coal. The D&RGW has been operating two of these trains each week -- in conjunction with similar trains moving coal from the Somerset mine, west of Paonia, Colorado. These trains are merged together at Grand Junction, and from there to their ultimate destination at the steel mills of Geneva, Utah, they operate as one train. Another unit train runs from Carbondale each week to Kaiser Steel in California, moving a somewhat smaller tonnage of coal than the trains going to U.S. Steel in Utah. The train in this picture is actually crossing a bridge over the Roaring Fork River, although the dense vegetation hides the river from view. In the background, Mount Sopris dominates the skyline, while in the foreground, sagebrush prevails over the scene.

PHOTO BY DELL A. MCCOY

In 1885, the village of Satank, Colorado, was situated at the confluence of the Crystal and Roaring Fork rivers. At this time the speediest form of transport for passengers and mail was the stagecoach. The railroads were laying track through western Colorado, but had not yet reached this point. This settlement was later replaced with Carbondale, located a short distance away. The Ed Dickinsol Stage Line was in business here, as can be seen from this photo. Near the coach, some of the local residents posed for the photographer -- attired in their best Sunday finery. The photographer was looking toward the northeast.

After the Meeker Massacre of September 20, 1879, soldiers pursued the Utes, which were led by Colorow and Buckskin Charlie. The Utes came up the Crystal River Valley and made their exit by way of Yule Pass. In the vicinity of Marble, they set fire to the forest so that wild game was driven before them, leaving no food for the soldiers. The fire damage may be the cause for the devastating snow slides that annually occur in and around Marble.

Another Ute incident took place during the Hayden Survey in the winter of 1874. The Hayden party was attacked on Sheep Mountain by a band of Utes, resulting in the deaths of several of the members. Following the attack, the survivors made their escape over McClures Pass. As late as 1914, one member of the party came into Marble to relate his terrible experience.

"Captain Jacks", a lady miner, owned the Black Queen Mine above Marble in 1870. About that time a war party of Utes passed through. One brave lost his life by "Captain Jack's" accuracy as a dead shot when the brave attempted to scalp her. She carried the scar the rest of her life. About 13 braves were killed at this time which happened about the time of the Hayden Survey.

In 1863, the Ute nation signed away much of what was then still considered eastern Utah (Utah being the name given to the land of the Ute Indians). In exchange, the Utes got supposedly permanent reservation lands, of which the Crystal River Valley was a part, ". . . for as long as the rivers might run and the grasses might grow." However, due to white man's greed and covetousness, the Ute

nation was forcibly marched off to southwestern Colorado and northern Utah in 1881.

Some of the earliest printed record concerning the Crystal River district began during the 1880's in "The Crystal River Current," Crystal City's newspaper. Silver and gold mining were the rage during this period, and the talk of the day was for better transportation. Roads were nonexistent and trails were not suitable for wagon travel. During the long winter months, snowshoeing was often the only means of travel.

THE COLORADO & UTAH RAILWAY COMPANY

Incorporated July 9, 1886, the Colorado & Utah Railway Company decided to do something about the transportation problem in the Crystal River Valley. The railway was a paperwork road that made transactions on a grand manner to secure and clear ownership on a right-of-way from Carbondale to a point on Yule Creek and from the mouth to the head of Coal Creek.

One-million dollars of capital stock was authorized and $25,000.00 par value was issued to the Denver Fuel Company, predecessor of the Colorado Fuel and Iron Company. When this railway company was sold on November 29, 1892, C.F.&I. controled ownership through stock purchases.

The Crystal River Toll Road Company

The Crystal River Toll Road Company was incorporated on July 10, 1886, and had surveys made and acquired rights-of-way. Then began the work of building wagon roads and trails along the valley of the Crystal River. By June 25, 1887, a postoffice had been established at Carbondale and W. M. Dinkle was appointed postmaster. The village of Satank, sometimes called Yellow Dog, was then moved to Rockford, about two miles farther down the valley.

Prior to this, Colorado financier and founder of today's CF&I Steel Corp., J.C. Osgood, had done a great deal of exploring in the valley. From 1883 to 1886, he purchased large bodies of coal lands which were then sold to the Colorado Fuel & Iron Company (CF&I). In his letter to one George M. Forbes, dated August 1898, Mr. Osgood mentioned coal as the principal resource of the region. He had exhaustive experiments made on the coal in the ovens at Sopris, Colorado, and found that it produced superior coke to the Connellsville coke of Pennsylvania, both in structure and percentage of ash, cell space and toughness.

Farther up the valley, he remarked that there was a considerable deposit of anthracite coal, equal in extent to any holdings C. F. & I. had up to that time. At the upper end of the valley, on a branch stream called Yule Creek, he mentioned enormous deposits of marble-pure white statuary marble. Mr. Osgood had the marble examined by experts who were familiar with Carrara and other Italian marbles. They all pronounced the marble

CONTINUED ON NEXT PAGE

of the very finest quality, and considered it equal to the best Carrara marble. J. C. Osgood then secured the most available portions of the marble at the base of the mountain and on the banks of the stream, together with water power facilities, mill sites, etc.

At the Denver Exposition in September of 1887, the Colorado Midland Railroad displayed several marble samples from their claims on Yule Creek. This points up the extreme interest financiers had in the Crystal River Valley at this time.

THE ELK MOUNTAIN RAILWAY COMPANY

Incorporated on December 5, 1887, the Elk Mountain Railway Company acquired right-of-way extending from Sands to Prospect, Colorado, a distance of 31 miles. The grading and masonry had been completed by Orman & Crook, subcontractors, under the Pacific Contract Company, General Contractor. The grade closely followed the Crystal River, however, no record can be found that shows that rail was actually laid. On July 27, 1898, this railway grade was sold due to insufficient funds being available to complete the line. Today State Highway No. 133 generally follows along and on top of this grade.

In 1892, J. C. Osgood formed the Crystal River Land & Improvement Company and exhibited a block of marble at the Columbian Exposition from his quarry. Nothing much came of this venture, however, because Osgood's attentions were withdrawn due to the silver panic of 1893 and his ensuing problems relating to the control of C. F. & I.

During this same period, Col. Channing F. Meek came onto the scene as president of the Colorado Coal & Iron Company, 1890-1893, which consolidated into the Colorado Fuel & Iron Company, based at Pueblo, Colorado.

1892

"The Carbonate Weekly Chronicle," published in Leadville, stated that this railroad company, the C.R.R.Y., was an amalgamation of Colorado Coal and Iron Company, the Colorado Fuel Company, and the Grand River Coal and Coke Company.

In 1890 the Hollands ranch built a wagon road up through the Devil's Punch Bowl on the Crystal River above Marble and connected with Crested Butte. A stage line ran between Redstone and Crested Butte until 1899.

In 1891 the Colorado Marble & Mining Company was incorporated and attempted to lay a railroad grade into the Crystal River Valley. It was intended for the grade to follow Slate Creek out of Crested Butte and head over the pass to Yule Creek. About two miles of grade work may be found above the site of Pittsburgh, now a ghost town on the Crested Butte side of the pass. Work on the grade was reported in the "Silver Lance" for June 29, 1893. This company was in the process of opening the quarries on Yule Creek and had plans to furnish the marble for the State Capital Building at Denver.

November 12, 1892, the "Elk Mountain Pilot," a Crested Butte newspaper, reported that S. W. Keene had a crew of graders at work on the "Marble Road" out of Crested Butte. However, work was halted by a snowstorm a short time thereafter. On November 26, 1892, the paper reported the Colorado Marble Company camp was located on the divide between Slate River and Paradise Gulch. A little over two-and-one-fourth miles had been completed with sixty men employed. The grade was four per cent with a right-of-way 14 feet in width. The grade was about 1/4-mile from the top, just a short distance remained to the marble quarries. Work was expected to be completed in the spring.

November 28, 1893, the "Elk Mountain Pilot" reported that S. W. Keene has a mine in Mexico out of which he can take a few millions and he has enough marble "up there" to make tombstones for the world. The railway expected to use electric engines. Again work was stopped because of the snowstorm. The same paper reported on July 29, 1893, that Mr. Keene had 150 men working. No other reports were found on this railroad attempt.

Hoffman & Tischauseer built a smelter at Marble to process gold, silver, lead, and zinc ores in 1898. The owner's high expectations came to naught in a short time, however, and the smeltering operation was abandoned. The smelter failed in short time due to the poor grade of the ores in the district and the partner's lack of knowledge in operations.

ASPEN & WESTERN

ncorporated on June 7, 1886, the Aspen and Western Railway Company platted their terminal at Carbondale, Colorado. This enterprise was the first actual railroad to be constructed in the Crystal River Valley and was built at an expense of nearly $400,000. Part of the construction expense went for buildings: $4,930.00 for passenger and freight depots, $700.00 for a small engine house, and another $700.00 for a telegraph line. The rock work was very heavy. Plans included a roundhouse at Carbondale with four engine stalls, trackage to lead in from both Midland Railroad, and the Denver & Rio Grande Railway. Plans also included a blast furnace site, along with coke ovens at the north side of town. At this time the Colorado Coal & Iron Company, owners of the Aspen & Western, changed the name of Rock Creek to "Crystal River" to differentiate this river from the many others by the same name.

The Aspen & Western then began laying 40-pound rail over a 13-mile route from the survey line of the Denver & Rio Grande's on-coming track at Carbondale to Willow Park on Thompson Creek. The grading was completed in December 1887 and a mine drift was bored for several hundred yards into one of many coal seams found in the Huntsman Hills.

The Denver & Rio Grande played an important role in the development of the Aspen & Western Railway. Their interest was in securing extra freight tonnage and the possibility of merging the A. & W. with the Rio Grande system in later years.

The Colorado Coal & Iron Company acknowledged a bill from the D&RG April 6, 1888, for the sum of $86,628.30, for the construction of the Aspen & Western Railway. The D&RG constructed items such as the telegraph line, water tank, turntable, station building, and section house. These items were probably built at Willow Park. The letter also noted that cuts and banks had been widened for future use of standard gauge operations. An agreement drawn up on January 14, 1888, between the D&RG and the A&W, stated the D&RG furnished all the steel rail, spikes, bolts, and splices used on the grade. The Aspen & Western furnished the iron bridges. The D&RG was to furnish all rolling stock for a period of five years. The agreement also stated that plans included coke ovens at Willow Park. The output of the coal mines was stated to amount to 150-tons per day. Also noted in this document was the existence of a tram line at Willow Park that ran to the coal mines. This may have been necessary because of the increase in grade above Willow Park and one very tight curve of about forty degrees. The agreement was duly signed by David H. Moffat, president of the D&RG, and Henry Sprague, president of the A&W.

Robert Sewell, born at Thompson Creek, remembers seeing in 1888 only one Aspen & Western train passing the ranch on its way to the coal mines at Willow Park. One hundred thirteen tons of coal were hauled out on this train. It probably consisted of a leased Denver & Rio Grande narrow gauge locomotive, four to six gondolas and a caboose. The Aspen & Western was sold on November 29, 1892, having an existence of about six years. The wood bridges and rail were then removed and used on the Crystal River Railroad, the rail going to Redstone for use on the coke oven sidings and bridges on the Coalbasin Branch.

A letter written to George M. Forbes by J. C. Osgood, in August of 1898, tells that the Colorado Coal & Iron Company -- with their usual lack of foresight -- had failed to adequately prospect before building their road, and after they built the road they found that the veins at that point were in bad condition and they were not justified in opening the mines or building ovens. They therefore dropped the enterprise early in 1889.

Aspen & Western Railway

MAP LEGEND:
- ASPEN & WESTERN RAILWAY
- TRAM GRADE
- ELK MOUNTAIN RAILWAY GRADE
- CRYSTAL RIVER RAILROAD

CRYSTAL RIVER RAILROAD (1898)

CRYSTAL RIVER RAILWAY (1893)

GRUBBS

SEWELL

ASPEN & WESTERN RAILWAY

CARBONDALE

CRYSTAL RIVER

ELK MOUNTAIN RAILWAY GRADE

GARFIELD COUNTY
PITKIN COUNTY

0   1/
SCALE OF MILES

ASPEN & WESTERN RAILWAY

TRACK AND BRIDGES OUT IN 1893

THOMPSON CREEK

ROAD

WILLOW PARK

COAL MINE

COAL MINE

THE COLORADO COAL & IRON COMPANY.

MINERS AND MAKERS OF

COAL AND COKE

MANUFACTURERS OF

STEEL RAILS, IRON & NAILS.

COALS:
CANON.
WALSEN.
EL MORO.
CRESTED BUTTE.

COKE:
EL MORO.
CRESTED BUTTE.

STEEL RAILS,
PIG IRON.
BAR IRON.
MINE RAILS.
SPLICE BARS, SPIKES.
BOLTS & NUTS.
NAILS.
CAST IRON PIPE.

Copy made

SALES AGENCY, DENVER, COLORADO

GENERAL OFFICE, SOUTH PUEBLO, COLO.

Denver, Colo., April 6th 1888 /88/

W.G. BROWN.
GENERAL AGENT.

S. T. Smith Esq.,

General Manager, D.&.R.G.R.R.Co., Denver.

Dear Sir: We have your bill for work done by your Company

in completion of Aspen and Western Railway, and the items of

actual expense amounting to $86,628.30 are all right, subject

to checking of our Superintendent and the credits named in my

former letters to you. Regarding the items of estimate named

on last page of bill would say as follows; On construction of

telegraph line we should only be required to pay the cost of

_____ting the same as that is all you were _____ding the items of

14

This townsite plat of Carbondale, published c. 1886, shows the ambitious plans that the Aspen & Western Railway had for promoting their coal mining operations located in the scenic Thompson Creek Canyon. The plan clearly shows a blast furnace site and a track for coke ovens, neither of which was ever built. Also notice the projected lines of other railroads which were never built. Although an A&W line was projected to connect with the Colorado Midland, the only interchange ever built was with the Denver & Rio Grande.

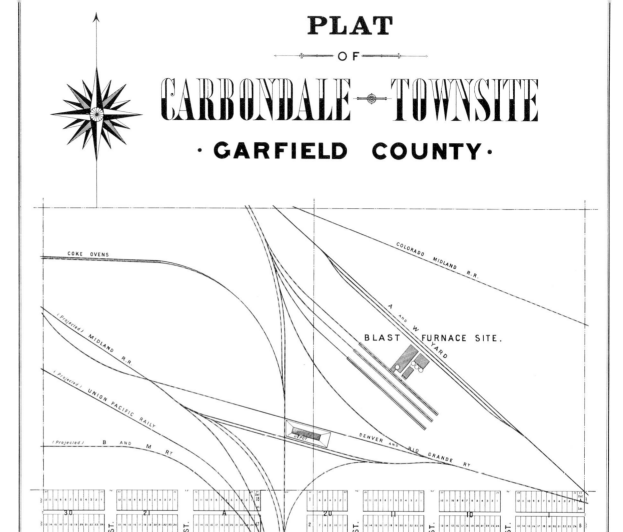

PLAT
OF
CARBONDALE ⚹ TOWNSITE
· GARFIELD COUNTY ·

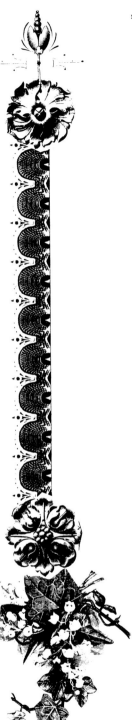

A train trip over the Aspen & Western right of way would have proved to be most inspiring. The river canyon the railroad followed was not only remote, but was quite scenic. Leaving the depot grounds at Carbondale, Colorado, the roadbed headed south toward the Crystal River, crossed and followed the river for about three miles at a widening distance. Upon reaching Thompson Creek, a curve led the trackage into the canyon about 30 feet above the creek. The train would have clattered along at a steady -- if somewhat slow pace -- with many fine examples of cottonwoods, willows and conifers filling the scene, along with arid-region plants. The grade runs at a steady one-percent or better for most of the trip. About seven miles from Carbondale, the roadbed swings to the south, crossing another small creek. At this point, the scenery has few rivals for spectacular rock formations – in reds and tans -- reaching crumbling fingers heavenward. Rounding another curve to the west, Willow Park opens up. Here the track made a "figure eight" curve, climbing at about 4 percent up along up the hillside and through several cuts. Rails still lie beneath the silt here. The coal mine portal was at the end of a siding paralleled by several sod roofed log cabins which had been built to house the miners. One grade continued for about a mile to another mine drift.

COLLECTION OF MICHAEL KOCH

The Elk Mountain Railway, according to the letter on the following page, was setting up a meeting with the D&RG to locate a site for the Elk Mountain depot. The second letter warns the D&RG about the land they are dealing with as belonging to The Colorado Coal & Iron Company. This iron company later built the Aspen & Western Railway, which later became the site of the Crystal River Railway.

ASPEN & WESTERN PASS SIGNED BY CHANNING F. MEEK

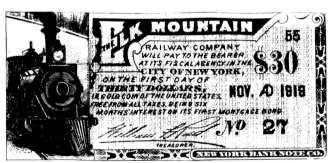

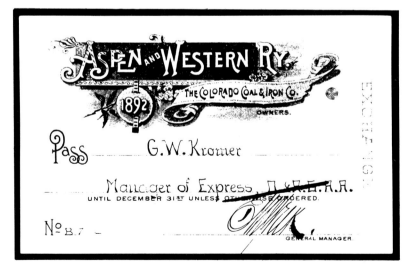

COLLECTION OF MORRIS ABBOTT

WESTERN COLLECTION, DENVER PUBLIC LIBRARY

THE ELK MOUNTAIN RAILWAY CO.

OF COLORADO.

PRESIDENT'S OFFICE.

Colorado Springs 13/3/ 1889

RECEIVED
MAR 14 1889
Chief Engineers Office
D. & R. G. R. R.

R. C. Briggs Esq
Chief Engineer
D. R. G. Ry

Dear Sir:

Can you inform us here at what time you will be able to go over to Carbondale, to look over the ground of Mrs Cooper, in order to select the best point for depot grounds &c.? As I understand, Judge Rennet & Mrs Cooper have been over, have seen you in regard to it.   I shall have to go over soon anyway, and will have to go up as far as Crystal, and I would like to get this depot biz finished before getting away beyond communication.

Yrs very truly Frank P. Wood

Legal Dept. Form No. 1.   SUBJECT:

THE COLORADO COAL & IRON COMPANY.

LEGAL DEPARTMENT.

Pueblo, Colorado,   January 24th,   1891.

C. STECK,
ATTORNEY.

W. A. Duel, Esq., Spt.,

   D. & R. G. R. R. Co.,

      B u i l d i n g:

Dear Sir:

   I understand that your company is negotiating with Mr. Isaac Vossler, of Carbondale, for an additional right of way; and in connection therewith I desire to advise and notify you that the property through which your line of railway runs, as also the additional ground which you propose to secure, is of the property of this company; and that Mr. Vossler has no right, title or interest therein.

   I had this matter up sometime since with Mxx Wolcott & Vail, and so advised them.   Will you please govern yourself accordingly?

      Yours truly,

            Attorney.

17

The construction camp of the Aspen & Western Railway was located about one mile up Thompson Creek Canyon, due west of the Crystal River. This rare old photo shows the log dwellings used for the grading crew's quarters, blacksmith shop, kitchen and dining facilities. During the summer of 1887, the crew completed tracklaying to Willow Park, a distance of 13 miles. In 1888, at least 113-tons of coal were brought out before the project was shut down (in 1889). Carbondale was the terminus of this narrow gauge railroad.

Mr. C. B. Sewell is shown here on his property next to the Aspen & Western grade, proudly displaying five-pound potatoes he grew in 1909. The log cabin was typical of dwellings found in this region during the early days of settlement.

PHOTO BY A. L. BEEKLY, COURTESY OF THE U.S. GEOLOGICAL SURVEY

The forces of Nature slowly but inevitably wear away at the meticulously crafted stone work in Thompson Creek Canyon. The wooden Pratt-type bridge that once rested on this abutment had long been removed to serve the narrow gauge Coalbasin Branch of the Crystal River Railroad before 1900.

PHOTO BY TRUMAN YOUNG

A pioneer who once lived at the entrance to Thompson Creek Canyon is shown below posing for his picture with rifle in hand. Just behind this old-timer may be seen a glimpse of the Aspen & Western grade.

In October of 1963, the Aspen & Western grade was still visible -- as this view attests -- looking down Thompson Creek toward the east. The telegraph pole placed there in 1887 tilts away from the grade at a cock-eyed angle. The red-rock formations are quite spectacular at this point. Further west, the rock colorings vary from reddish-brown to golden-tan. The right-of-way curves to the south here.

The last stonework built along the grade of the Aspen & Western held a bridge span which crossed the North Fork of Thompson Creek, here about seven miles out of Carbondale. This autumn view, taken in 1966, shows some of the variety of vegetation found in Colorado. As elevation increases, the types of plantlife changes. The aspen -- a type of poplar tree -- flourishes at the higher altitudes of the state and is common throughout much of the Crystal River district. In the fall the creek runs low and clear, but during the spring and summer, when rainfall is more abundant, the stream flow is greater and the water is often roily.

PHOTO BY A. L. BEEKLY
COURTESY OF U.S. GEOLOGICAL SURVEY

Loaded with supplies for their winter quarters, these old-time ranchers head for the Middle Thompson Creek on October 15, 1909. This view shows the cowboys entering Willow Park over the Aspen & Western grade.

Farther up the canyon, the A&W crossed Middle Thompson Creek over a wooden trestle, part of which has withstood the rise and fall of creek waters since 1887. Notice the tree bark still clinging to logs in this photo taken in 1966.

PHOTO BY TRUMAN YOUNG

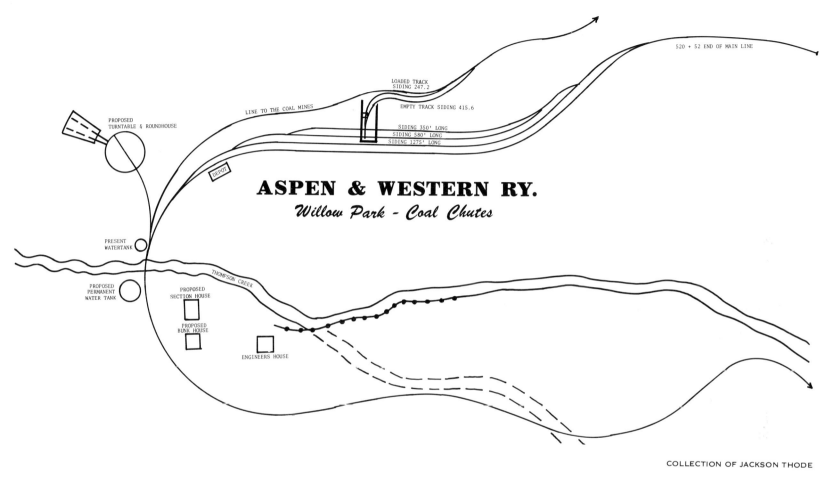

520 + 52 END OF MAIN LINE

LOADED TRACK
SIDING 247.2

LINE TO THE COAL MINES

EMPTY TRACK SIDING 415.6

SIDING 350' LONG
SIDING 580' LONG
SIDING 1275' LONG

PROPOSED
TURNTABLE & ROUNDHOUSE

DEPOT

ASPEN & WESTERN RY.

Willow Park - Coal Chutes

PRESENT
WATERTANK

THOMPSON CREEK

PROPOSED
PERMANENT
WATER TANK

PROPOSED
SECTION HOUSE

PROPOSED
BUNK HOUSE

ENGINEERS HOUSE

COLLECTION OF JACKSON THODE

The promoters of the Aspen & Western planned a terminal at Willow Park, as shown in this detailed track sketch. Taken from an original pencil sketch, officially stamped "received March 24, 1888," this reproduction has been re-drawn to improve clarity. Plans may have included a steam-donkey tram operation on the branch line to the coal mines. This grade increased to about 4-percent at this point. There was one sharp curve along this route that may have exceeded 60-degrees.

As may be expected of narrow gauge railroads in Colorado, the Aspen & Western had a portion of very steep grade -- probably four-percent -- and curvature of very sharp radius, as seen in the photo to the left. Photographed in 1966, the grade enters the picture from the left, from Willow Park. It climbs and goes through an "S" curve, then ascends the hillside in the distance, turns through a cut and proceeds through several more cuts, finally arriving at the coal mine.

PHOTO BY TRUMAN YOUNG

PHOTO BY TRUMAN YOUNG

In all likelyhood, the Aspen & Western trackage terminated at this coal mine opening -- situated about a mile beyond several other coal mine openings. Records indicate that 113-tons of coal were all that came from these mines, while under control of the Colorado Coal & Iron Company.

Down by the Carbondale Depot

N

D&RG RAILROAD MAINLINE

LUMBER SPUR

INDUSTRY SPUR

CRYSTAL RIVER RAILROAD

Carbondale

CARBONDALE

PHOTO BY RICHARD KINDIG

A short time before Dick Kindig shot this station scene, the Denver & Rio Grande Western's local freight train had pulled out of Carbondale, heading for Glenwood Springs. Meanwhile CR&SJ 2-6-0 Number 2 coupled onto combine Number 9 -- ready for the return trip to Marble. Notice the spark arrestor on the engine's stack -- normally in use only during the dry season. Photographed on July 4, 1940.

CARBONDALE & MT SOPRIS   SEP 1908

CRYSTAL RIVER – *The Columbine Route*

Incorporated on August 8, 1892, this company was formed to join together into one the properties of the Elk Mountain Railway Company, The Aspen & Western Railway Company, The Colorado & Utah Railway Company and the Crystal River Toll Road Company. This line was controlled by the Colorado Fuel & Iron Corporation of which J. C. Osgood was in control. The railway began at the Denver & Rio Grande depot in Carbondale and proceeded over the right-of-way of the Aspen & Western for about three miles. The railway then followed along the east bank of the Crystal River to a point near Hot Springs, a distance of 13

Looking toward the south, Mount Sopris shows off her snow-capped mantle -- reaching an altitude of 12,823-ft. above sea level. Below the peak, at an elevation of 6,181 ft., Carbondale basks in the late afternoon sun. The year was 1906 -- the Crystal River Railroad's peak year in business. Carbondale's population was about 500 persons at this time. This farm and ranch supply center served as the Crystal River Railroad's northern terminus; the routes of both the Crystal River and the Denver & Rio Grande railroads being plainly visible in this view. The river in the foreground is the Roaring Fork River, a tributary of the Colorado River.

miles, of which 9 miles had belonged to the Crystal River Toll Road Co. Much heavy grading was done on what was to become the Coalbasin Branch at this time. About 3 miles of Elk Mountain property was used in construction between Avalanche and Placita. Rail used was 57#. The standard gauge railway did not exceed 2-1/2 per cent grades between Carbondale and Hot Springs. At this time the Crystal River Ry. planned to extend the line to Marble for the marble deposits near there and then to extend on into Crystal City to tap the ore traffic from the nearby districts.

J. C. Osgood had a Coal Company at Crystal City at this time and it was necessary to freight in this coal and hay by burro sometimes numbering 75 from Crested Butte.

On April 29, 1893, the "Elk Mountain Pilot" newspaper of Crested Butte reported that the Crystal River Railway had 10 miles of track, both standard gauge and narrow gauge.

The "Elk Mountain Pilot" of Saturday, September 3, 1893, reported that the Crystal River Railway had seven miles of track operating. On Monday, the Crystal River got their 60-ton standard gauge engine. "A very considerable amount of work has already been done with only a narrow gauge engine rented from the R. G. S.

The brave little narrow gauge engine has had more than it could possibly do at times to pull the long string of cars and has had to have help on the third rail by some one of the Rio Grande broad gauge engines." The narrow gauge engine reported here was probably Number 11, purchased new by the Crystal River in 1893.

The only conclusion the writers can come to regarding this dual-gauge track is that it began at Carbondale, Colorado, on the grade of the abandoned Aspen & Western and proceeded out of town for two miles. There the track left the Aspen & Western and continued on toward Redstone. The Aspen & Western was narrow gauge and the Crystal River Railway probably laid enough standard gauge ties in the grade to add rails to the outside of the existing three-foot gauge track to make standard gauge train movements possible. Narrow gauge freight cars were in abundance at this time and the Crystal River Railway probably used some of these for construction of the line.

The heavy fall in the price of Silver caused many smelters to shut down after 1893 and greatly reduced the use of coke. Since the Crystal River Railway's primary purpose was to transport coal and coke, the railway then shut down for about five years, along with construction activities

SECTION III CONTINUED ON PAGE 29

Mid-Continent Coal and Coke Co. of Carbondale is now the big business enterprise of the Crystal River Valley. The U. S. Steel, "Unit Train" is shown loading at the tipple. The drop bottom hoppers drift slowly under the chute as the crushed coal rides on a belt system from the holding bin to the far left. This train hauls out 5,000 tons per trip.

of the coal mine at Coal Basin and beehive coking at Redstone.

An excellent traffic contract was signed by the Denver & Rio Grande R.R. and the C.R.RR. dealing with the use of freight cars and interchange tonnage. This connection was to run for a period of fifty years. Another favorable factor of this railway was that the Colorado Midland passed within two miles of Carbondale and could be used as an additional connection. By March 16, 1893, the Crystal River Railway was reported to have been completed to Hot Springs. The road was then sold on Sept. 13, 1898, with no record of having run a revenue train.

CRYSTAL RIVER RAILROAD COMPANY

Incorporated on September 6, 1898, the reorganized Crystal River Railroad Co. purchased the holdings of the Crystal River Railway. The road was controlled by Colorado Fuel & Iron Corp. All operations then ceased on December 7, 1919. The property then lay idle until April 5, 1922 when it was operated under lease by Crystal River and San Juan Railroad. Many land titles and holdings had probably changed with the complications of the silver panic, and C. F. & I. probably thought it advisable to re-establish their railway into a railroad. The railroad then went into operation July 1, 1899.

The Crystal River Railroad consisted of a single track standard gauge main line running from Carbondale, Colorado, to Placita, Colorado, a distance of 20.6 miles. The Placita depot sign read, "20.1 miles from Carbondale". The track extended three-fourths of a mile past the depot. The Coalbasin Branch -- or "High Line" as it was called -- was built to three-foot narrow gauge and was completed on November 22, 1900. In 1898, the rails reached Redstone. In 1902, some 75-pound steel was laid in the main line.

A RAILROAD TRIP FROM CARBONDALE TO COALBASIN

In 1906, a traveler from other regions could arrive by train from over the D&RG through Glenwood Springs, Colorado, arriving at Carbondale at 10:34 a.m. The Crystal River Railroad train would then leave Carbondale at 11:00 a.m., having coupled on cars of merchandise and empty gondolas for shippers up the line. Passengers would board a combine coach immaculately painted in olive green. Two short whistle blasts and the train would leave Carbondale, heading south past green fields, stopping on occasion to drop empties for potatoe loading at short sidings along the way. Climbing a steady 1-percent grade, the train would then enter the narrowing canyon where the river closed up next to the roadbed about four-miles out of Carbondale. To the right, Thompson Creek empties into the Crystal River. The Aspen & Western trackage followed along Thompson Creek from this point due west.

Approaching West Needle Creek, the train would pull to a stop for water at a stand pipe. Whistling off, engine Number 1, named the "Bull of the Woods," would then round "Red Wind Point" and would come into the small settlement of Janeway just before noon.

Janeway was situated in a small park -- about 10.5-miles south of Carbondale -- with the Crystal River flowing past on the west. The commercial buildings of this village housed a store, saloon and post office. This was an important stopover for teamsters on their way to the high country where they would load ore. Janeway had a siding for 29 cars that could have handled ore shipments from the nearby districts located up Avalanche Creek.

Whistling off at the depot at 11:53 a.m., engine Number 1 would then pull her train over two small bridges and round a curve through a narrow cut and proceed into the narrow canyon. The engine would work harder due to the increased grade of 2.2-percent from here on into Redstone. Passengers could see a higher grade at this point, constructed by the Burlington Railroad before the Crystal River Railway began construction. About 1927 the Mormon Church quarried stone from here for a short period of time, and loaded at the north end of this grade onto the Crystal River Railroad with the use of a one car spur.

Emerging from the canyon, the valley again opens up at Hot Springs. These springs are said to be equal to those of Glenwood in healing and restorative power. For many years this was known as Penny Hot Springs, after the caretaker that lived there with his family. A boarding house and caretakers' buildings were situated here along with a small concrete bath in a wood building beside the Crys-

CONTINUED ON NEXT PAGE

tal River. The bathhouse was partitioned into two parts to separate the ladies from the gents. Submerging underwater would have been most revealing since the partition stopped at water height.

At 12:25 the train would have arrived at Redstone, superintendent's headquarters for both standard and narrow gauge, elevation 7,200-feet. Uncoupling from the combine coach, engine Number 1 would then have gone about her switching duties, depositing empties at the upper end of the yard and making up a train of loaded coal and box cars of coke to be shipped out. Having completed switching duties, engine Number 1 would have put together a train and headed for Placita to service the coal mine there.

Meanwhile, one of the narrow gauge locomotives would have dropped down from the roundhouse with the bright red waycar to pick up passengers at the Redstone depot. This was an unusual and interesting combination caboose and passenger car -- of a type used on both the C&W and the CR. Heading for Coalbasin, the little engine would have whistled off at 1:30 p.m. and backed up the main line past the interchange turnout. The dual-gauge trackage continued on up the interchange, enabling engines of both gauges to shunt coal cars over the tipple. Passing the tipple loop, the waycar would be dropped momentarily so that the engine could back into the loop and couple onto the empty Ingoldsby dump cars. Link and pin coupling was used on the narrow gauge until abandonment.

Gathered into a mixed train, the travelers would then enjoy the pleasures of a trip up the 4.3-percent grade to Coalbasin. Curving constantly, the track straightened out at only one place long enough so that a train of thirteen cars could be in a straight line. Owing to the extreme grade, a train of seven empties taxed Numbers 101 and 102 engines to their maximum. Purchased in 1902, Number 103 was larger than the other consolidations and could handle 10 empties. Entering a narrow red rock canyon, Coal Creek flowed closely to the grade. Halfway to Coalbasin the track made large figure eight loops and climbed into a small meadow. Here the track looped back and forth, crossed the creek, climbed over the meadow through cuts and headed westward, out onto a breathtaking view with beaver ponds far below. J. C. Osgood called the line the "Columbine Road" which one can understand from the outstanding flower displays along the way. The nickname was also a play on the railway's initials, C.R. -- the initials were worked into an elaborate company herald (emblem).

At Medio, an upgrade train would normally pass the waiting downgrade train. A small settlement was situated here on the bank of Coal Creek. Leaving Medio, the train then climbed up through thick forest and began figure eight loops again of very sharp 40-degree curves. The diameter of these curves would measure about 300-feet for a curve of this degree. At this point a striking vista of the Continental Divide was viewed at every turn, and passengers could look down on the loops that they had just previously traversed.

Entering Coalbasin at an elevation of 9,500-feet, the train would have rumbled into what was one of Colorado's highest coal mining camps. Bubbling brooklets, waterfalls, gushing springs and to the east the distant peaks of the Elk Mountain Range -- perpetually crowned with snow -- could not help but excite admiration, wonder and awe. The forests abounded with all varieties of game found in the Rockies. Being protected on the north, west and south by mountains, Coalbasin is screened from severe storms, wind and blizzards that would otherwise have been a menace because of the heavy snowfall there.

Coalbasin was said to have but three seasons: Winter, July and August.

Passing under the mine's tramway trestle -- which stretched 1,400-feet up the mountainside -- the train would have stopped at the depot at 2:40 p.m., 11.38 miles from Redstone. The mine operated with a gravity trestle for the first years, with ten pit cars per trip. The loaded pit cars would travel down the trestle hoisting ten empties up to the mine by gravity. This was later changed to steam-cable funicular operation handling twenty cars each way. Run-of-mine coal was then loaded into Ingoldsby patent dump cars and hauled to Redstone to be screened. The lump coal was then shipped to railroads, mining and smelting operations. The slack went to the ovens at Redstone to be made into coke. In 1903, up to 25,000-tons of coal came out. Horses and mules were used inside the mine.

Coal was discovered at Coalbasin by C. D. Griffith and W. D. Perry in 1881 and about 1883, J. C. Osgood purchased large bodies of these coal lands for C. F. & I. The coal was tested in the C. F. & I. ovens at Sopris, Colorado, and it was

CONTINUED ON PAGE 32

DENVER & RIO GRANDE WESTERN						
	357		STATIONS		356	
lv.	9:40	a.m.	GLENWOOD	lv.	9:15	p.m.
"	10:34	"	CARBONDALE	"	8:22	"
"	11:08	"	EMMA	"	7:47	"
"	11:45	"	WOODY CREEK	"	7:10	"
"	12:20	p.m.	ASPEN	"	6:35	"
	FEB. 1, 1906					

The first engine purchased by the Crystal River Railway was Number 11, a 3-foot narrow gauge locomotive. Here she is shown on the Southern Iron & Equipment Company's transfer table at Atlanta, Georgia. This locomotive was purchased in 1893 as an 0-8-0 and was returned to Baldwin in 1894 where a 2-wheel pilot truck was installed. She then went through several owners and now reportedly rests in Cuba waiting for clearance to the United States for her latest owner (who recently died).

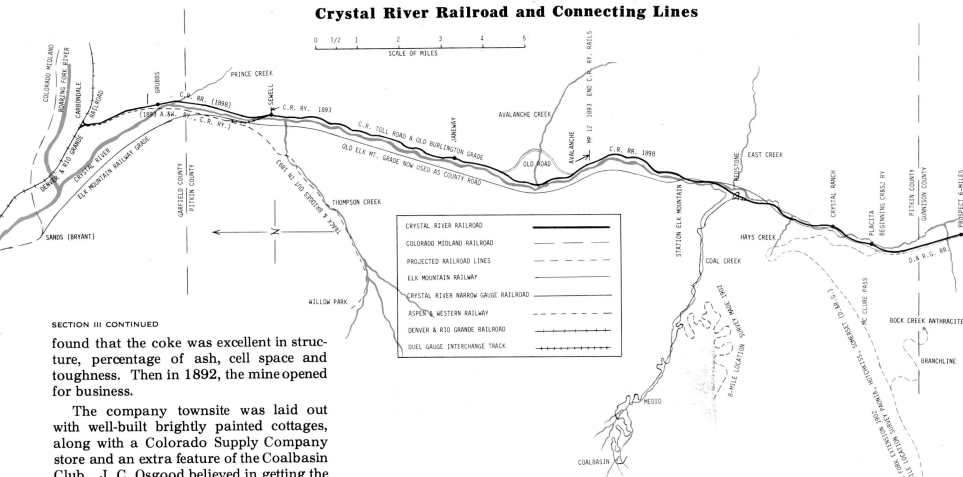

SCALE OF MILES
0 1/2 1 2 3 4 5

CRYSTAL RIVER RAILROAD
COLORADO MIDLAND RAILROAD
PROJECTED RAILROAD LINES
ELK MOUNTAIN RAILWAY
CRYSTAL RIVER NARROW GAUGE RAILROAD
ASPEN & WESTERN RAILWAY
DENVER & RIO GRANDE RAILROAD
DUEL GAUGE INTERCHANGE TRACK

SECTION III CONTINUED

found that the coke was excellent in structure, percentage of ash, cell space and toughness. Then in 1892, the mine opened for business.

The company townsite was laid out with well-built brightly painted cottages, along with a Colorado Supply Company store and an extra feature of the Coalbasin Club. J. C. Osgood believed in getting the most production from his workers by providing incentives, especially since the townsite was so isolated. Boxing clubs, orchestra and glee clubs, baseball and ice skating were the recreation of the day. Most residents were Austrians and Italians and about 265 men were employed. Many earned $105 to $135 per month in 1902.

One ride by push car down the narrow gauge branch was made in 22-minutes. Many times, Coalbasinites would beat the train down to Medio on foot by way of a short cut down the mountain side. Leaving

Coalbasin at 3:40 p.m., the train would have descended to Redstone, arriving at the depot at 5:00 p.m. The standard gauge train Number 2, pulled by big Number 1 would pull out of Redstone at 6:20 p.m. with the mixed freight and passenger train. Loads of potatoes would be picked up and the Crystal River Railroad would arrive at Carbondale 7:35 p.m. At 8:22 p.m. passengers could then have departed over the D&RG for the outside world.

Snow fighting was a costly item on the

"High Line". One storm closed the line for 22 days. The miners were called upon to trench down to the rail every six-feet so the rotary could bite through. This rotary was normally stored on a spur near the covered turntable at Coalbasin, so that it could work downgrade with the added help of gravity. The easternmost roundhouse stall at Redstone had a transfer pit so that standard gauge trucks could be placed under the rotary and the line to

Carbondale could be plowed open if the need arose.

REDSTONE

Shortly after the Silver Panic of 1893, activity began at Redstone. This was chosen as the site to transfer narrow gauge carloads of coal to the standard gauge cars, and for producing coke from Coalbasin coal. Two rows of beehive coke ovens were constructed along with a coal washer and a screening plant. The tipple contained the slack bin where larry cars were four-wheel wagons, which held five to six-tons of slack coal each, were loaded for charging the ovens. These cars were standard gauge and were pulled by mules. T. M. Gibb was named as superintendent of the coke plant. He substituted stream power for steam to run electricity at the tipple. Coke loadings averaged 11,000-tons per month.

JOHN C. OSGOOD

When J. C. Osgood first came into the valley, he set up his residence at the Crystal River Ranch on the hillside west of the river. Then the ranch was developed as his second residence -- primarily as a summer place. A two-car siding was placed there for his private car, "Sunrise", and a diner with a Negro porter and a cook with a peg leg. Many times J. C. Osgood would arrive in Redstone aboard the "Sunrise". Cleveholm was built as his third residence c. 1903, the last major construction to take place in Redstone.

REDSTONE VIGNETTES

To bring a better way of life to the common worker, J. C. Osgood had built a large club house of brick with an auditorium seating three hundred. Across the street on this hillside was located the village fire house equipped with a hand-drawn pumper. The Happy Hooligan Minstrels and the Redstone Band practiced with instruments furnished by J. C. Osgood in the second story of the firehouse. An interesting event occurred in 1903 when a fire alarm was turned in from the roundhouse at 3:00 a.m. one morning. About 20 members of the five crews responded, and as the hose could not be put into use, the water pipes to the roundhouse being frozen up, only the chemical engine was taken out. The snow was deep, and the night stormy, but the boys heroically tugged away, and finally arrived at the scene of the fire with 200-pounds pressure in the cylinder. The carbon dioxide gas made short work of the fire that resisted the efforts of Gibb's bucket brigade, and the blaze was confined to the boiler house in which it started and which was totally destroyed, together with several barrels of oil. The roundhouse – though immediately adjoining -- was saved, all but for a few hundred dollars damage. Had it not been for the chemical engine and the pertinacity of the crew, the roundhouse would have gone up in smoke.

A small brick schoolhouse was situated on the hillside and at the south end of town the Elk Mountain Inn was completed by Christmas of 1901 to house the bachelor workmen. Near this was located the Colorado Supply Company store and an ice house barn at the rear. Across the river, the doctor's office was located in the building beside the depot. A wash house was built near this for the coke workers to shower before going to their cottages. Up the hillside behind the coke ovens the Big Horn Lodge was built. This was intended to be used for fancy banquets with all the trimmings. One of its features was the bowling alley. Its use was limited because of the unpleasant smoke from the nearby ovens. Nearby, the villagers had garden plots and each family had a milk cow that was housed in a large barn there.

Redstone had a very pleasant atmosphere about it with Mount Sopris visible to the north and Chair Mountain rising to the south. The streets were tree-lined with native cottonwoods, spruce and aspen. Lake Gibb was formed near the bridge on the Crystal River.

The "1901 Christmas Grand Ball" was held at the Colorado Supply Company store. The Mandolin Club met twice a week. The bandstand was erected and the "Redstone 9's" baseball team was formed. Workmen attended night school to further their education. The Crystal River Fife and Drum Corps – with 29 instruments -- was formed in 1902. J. C. Osgood would furnish the kids presents hung on a tree for Christmas.

On November 8, 1902, the tender of the Crystal River engine Number 1 coupled hard and destroyed the drawhead and buffer beam. The roundhouse force stayed on the job all night to make repairs. During a jarring coupling one day in Carbondale the stove upset inside the coach of the mixed train. It caught fire and badly damaged the car. In another incident, the main line coach was struck by a car loaded with stone. It was rebuilt and put back in service. Twenty-seven car loads of cattle were shipped from Placita in 1902.

SECTION III CONTINUED ON PAGE 36

The Crystal River & San Juan's "ten-wheeler," Number 1, eases back and couples onto the combine at Carbondale, Colorado, on October 25, 1941. The train will then leave the D&RGW main line, work its way around the wye and head south for Marble with three empty cars waybilled for the marble works.

PHOTO BY RICHARD KINDIG

PHOTO BY DELL H. GERBAZ

On a hot Fourth of July in 1940, CR&SJ combination coach Number 9 stands near the Carbondale depot. This car was purchased from the Claredon & Pittsford during the final years of the road's operation. It was then purchased by Rome Isler of Marble for $50, who finally sold it to an individual who burned it for scrap. Number 9 was originally built as a full passenger coach, and in later years was remodeled for baggage, l.c.l. freight and mail use. Packages, crates and mail sacks were loaded through the side door.

Originally equipped with narrow gauge trucks, this boxcar first saw service on the Crystal River Railroad's Coalbasin Branch. After the Crystal River Railroad ceased operation, No. 101 went into service on the CR&SJ -- with standard gauge trucks under her frame. When photographed a few years ago, the car body was resting in a Carbondale backyard -- still in relatively good condition.

The end came for Redstone in 1909, about the time the company store closed its doors, January 12, 1909. The post office stayed open until September 15, 1909, when it too closed. The railroad continued to operate until November 19, 1910, according to a conductor's book of the CR&SJ. Then December 8, 1910, the CR&SJ extended their run from Redstone to Carbondale. For about four years previous, the two railroads had interchanged freight and passengers at Redstone -- the CR&SJ making two runs per day to Redstone. The Coalbasin branch closed so suddenly January 12, 1909, that residents were forced to leave behind most of the furniture, stoves and other bulky items they could not get out in one trip. No known reason may be found to explain the sudden closing of the coal mine and coking plant operations that were the life of these hamlets. In later years, J. C. Osgood came back to his mansion many times trying without success to reopen the town. The Crystal River Railroad closed their books December 1, 1919.

The narrow gauge locos were shipped out of Redstone in 1914 according to the C&W Ledger.

Sale of locos 101, 102, 103 $12,782 -- 1917. Sale of 41 dump cars $9,238.97 -- 1918. Nos. 101, 102, 103 worth $30,408.69 -- 1917.

COLLECTION OF FRED AND JO MAZZULLA

This Denver & Rio Grande ten-wheeler -- Number 532 -- shown here at Palmer Lake, Colorado, in 1899, was purchased by the Crystal River & San Juan in 1915. The wheel arrangement of this 4-6-0 made it highly useful for fast inter-city passenger service. Once in service along the Crystal River, she was used for the tri-weekly mixed train -- pulling lowly freight cars and sporting a "hand-me-down" combine at the end of each train.

In from Marble with a stock extra on October 25, 1941 -- CR&SJ Number 1 sizzles to herself in the Carbondale yard after doing her switching duties. This 4-6-0 was formerly the D&RG's Number 532, as shown on the preceeding page.

PHOTOS BY RICHARD KINDIG

CRYSTAL RIVER & SAN JUAN
RAILROAD

In the upper view on this page, CR&SJ Number 2 is shown arriving in Carbondale, Colorado, with 12 loaded cars of livestock. This livestock extra had been loaded at Placita, 20 miles south of Redstone. In the lower view, Number 2 is busily switching the same train beside the Carbondale depot. The railway telegraph line can be seen positioned at one end of the depot roof. The lower photo clearly shows Number 2's homemade universal piston valve chamber. Photographed on July 4, 1940.

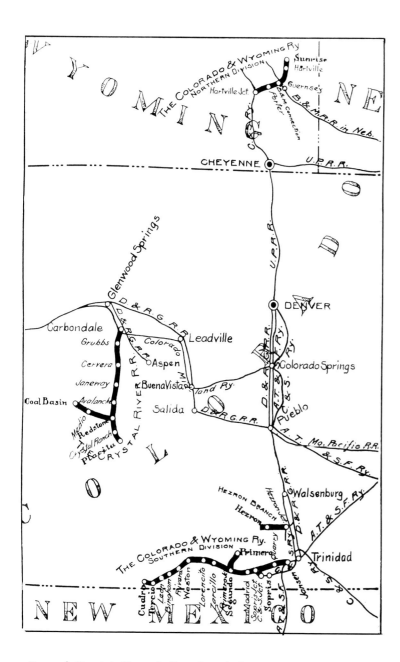

Map of Crystal River Railroad and the Colorado & Wyoming Railway, showing connections. Not to scale. Printed in "Camp and Plant" in 1901.

Locomotive Wheel Arrangement
Classification Chart

Symbol	Wheel Arrangement	Type
0-6-0		6-Wheel Switcher.
0-8-0		8-Wheel Switcher.
2-6-0		Mogul.
2-8-0		Consolidation.
4-6-0		10-Wheel.

CRYSTAL RIVER RAILROAD

	#1		STATIONS		#2	
lv.	11:00	a.m.	CARBONDALE	ar.	7:35	p.m.
"	11:07	"	GRABBS	lv.	7:30	"
"	11:32	"	SEWELL	"	7:18	"
"	11:53	"	JANEWAY	"	6:40	"
"	12:11	p.m.	AVALANCHE	"	6:30	"
ar.	12:25	"	REDSTONE	"	6:20	"
lv.	1:30	"	REDSTONE	ar.	5:00	"
ar.	2:40	"	COALBASIN	lv.	3:30	"

12-10-05

Both SG&NG daily except Sunday

Crystal River & San Juan "Mogul" Number 2 drifts downgrade into Carbondale on October 11, 1941, with the tri-weekly mixed train. In the background, Mount Sopris rises 6,000 feet above the valley floor. The Peak was named for Richard Sopris who explored the region in 1860 with fourteen companions from Denver. The gondolas in this train are loaded with marble, some of the last to come from the finishing plant at Marble.

This photograph shows CR&SJ Number 2 rattling downgrade into Janeway, September 6, 1941. Business was good in the last year of operation, requiring both engines to be used almost daily to handle marble shipments. The tender on engine Number 2 originally was sloped-backed. The extra section was added to carry more water. On many runs, the engine was short on water and the fire was killed just out of Marble. The train would drift on into town with steam pressure almost zero. The only stand pipe on the route was at Nettle Creek, near Janeway.

Morse Brothers Machinery Co. of Denver began salvage operations during the winter of 1941 -- after the I. C. C. had granted the CR&SJ permission for abandonment in the fall of 1941. A gas-powered railway spike-puller is being put to use in this view near Penny Hot Springs. The dismantling train can be seen further down the track.

During abandonment of the Crystal River & San Juan, flat car Number 201 was outfitted with a hoist engine mounted in the shack shown in this photo. The hoist was used to pull unspiked rails up onto the flat cars coupled behind the 201.

HARRIS COLLECTION

PHOTO BY MORRISON A. SMITH.   COLLECTION OF JOHN W. MAXWELL

41

The grade of the Crystal River Railway was often located quite close to the railway's namesake river -- as this dramatic 1959 Ektachrome clearly shows. The photographer was looking south, just below Penny Hot Springs. Railroad ties are still in place, as well as telegraph poles. The origin of the grade to the extreme left is believed to have been done by The Burlington Route before 1900. The Mormon Church hauled stone out from this slide rock area, c. 1927. Today the road has been paved and heavy coal trucks use it daily to haul loads from Coalbasin to a large storage tipple at Carbondale. At Carbondale, the Mid-Continent Coal & Coke Company loads Rio Grande 5,000-ton capacity unit trains for movement to the U. S. Steel mills at Geneva, Utah.

This station (view at right) on the CR&SJ was named "Manalta". The name was used during the last years of CR&SJ operations, during which time the line leased the right-of-way between Placita and Carbondale. When the Crystal River Railroad was in operation, the station was known as Sewell. Two cars could be spotted here on a stub siding usually used to load potatoes from rich farmlands on both sides of the river. The Crystal River is to the rear of the depot in this photo taken about 1912.

In 1922, the CR&SJ made an agreement with the D&RG to do maintenance work on the line in return for a guarantee of 1,500 cars of marble each year. A steam shovel -- mounted on rails on a flat car -- was used during one operation when the river had undercut the grade in several places. Hand shoveling was out of the question due to the severity of damage. The work shown here was being done north of Janeway

During the roadbed reconstruction, a side-dump hopper was first loaded at a convenient location along a hillside. Then the work train would back upgrade to the washed-out grade and dump the car. Notice the untreated ties used on the grade.

The engineer and fireman on the CR&SJ could not hang out of the cab while traveling through this narrow rock cut near Avalanche! Notice the frost on the engine's pilot and coupler this chilly winter day toward the end of the railroad's operations.

COLLECTION OF THE LATE WILLIAM MCMANUS

COLLECTION OF MRS. MAURINE BARNES HERMAN

COLLECTION OF EVERETT MURPHY

PHOTO BY DELL A. MCCOY

PHOTO BY DELL A. MCCOY

This view -- taken in the fall of 1971, near Avalanche -- shows the use the CR&SJ made of poor-grade marble for "rip-rapping" the banks of the Crystal River. The railroad grade is just above the marble. The water is muddy from a rainstorm the previous day.

Photographed in the fall of 1967, this color view shows the old stagecoach stop at Penny Hot Springs, north of Redstone. Stagecoach was the finest way of travel through the valley before the Crystal River Railway began to fling her iron up the valley in 1892. To the south, Chair Mountain comes into view in the distance.

Drifting down the 2.2-percent grade past Penny Hot Springs, CR&SJ Number 2 was hauling a boxcar of marble to Carbondale one day in 1935. Coach Number 9 was tacked on the rear for passenger and conductor usage. The hot springs bubbled up along-side the Crystal River at this point. Several old prospect holes on the hillsides show evidence of early-day mining attempts. However, the ore proved to be of low grade and the diggings were short lived. The mining activity took place before permanent settlers came into the valley. Penny Hot Springs was a moderately popular spa for a short time near the turn of the century -- when summer visitors took advantage of the warm mineral water. A fine guest house with dining facilities was built close to the track, while a bath house was right down next to the river.

Photographed at Redstone in 1911, the crew of 4-6-0 Number 701 takes a breather during re-railing of the engine. A jack has been placed under the pilot beam to raise the engine back onto the rail. This leased Colorado & Wyoming ten-wheeler was built mainly for passenger service.

Track Laying.

"Crystal River Railroad" was the emblem painted on the cab of engine Number 1, shown below at Redstone. A three-pocket link and pin set-up adorned her pilot, which enabled her to couple to both standard and narrow gauge cars. This Baldwin 2-8-0 locomotive was built in 1900. She was christened the "Bull-of-the-Woods" because of the unusual whistle an engineer had fitted to her. This whistle reportedly came off a Mississippi River steamboat and had a moan to it that sounded like "a bull about to break down an oak gate." When a "hogger" would call for the

COLLECTION OF ROBERT LEMASSENA

JOHN SMITH COLLECTION "CAMP AND PLANT" CF&I MAGAZINE

board at Redstone or Carbondale on night runs, the whistle would awaken everyone. Echoes would bounce off the rocky cliffs and moan back and forth as though the end of the world was near. The view above shows this same locomotive on the Southern Division of the Colorado & Wyoming as Number 7. This engine left the Crystal River for service on the C&W about 1906.

A. Taylor M. D. Crystal River
Railroad Surgeon, Redstone.

Photographed about 1915, this scene shows the doctor's office located beside the Redstone depot. Fall was in the air and it was time for moving livestock down from the high country. The automobile is one of Henry Ford's famous "Model T's".

When this photo was taken, a freight train of merchandise had just arrived in Redstone on a winter day during 1902. Passengers rode in the combination caboose-coach of the day. The third rail was used by the Crystal River Railroad's narrow gauge Coalbasin Branch to pick up and deliver passengers, l.c.l. freight, and mail at the depot.

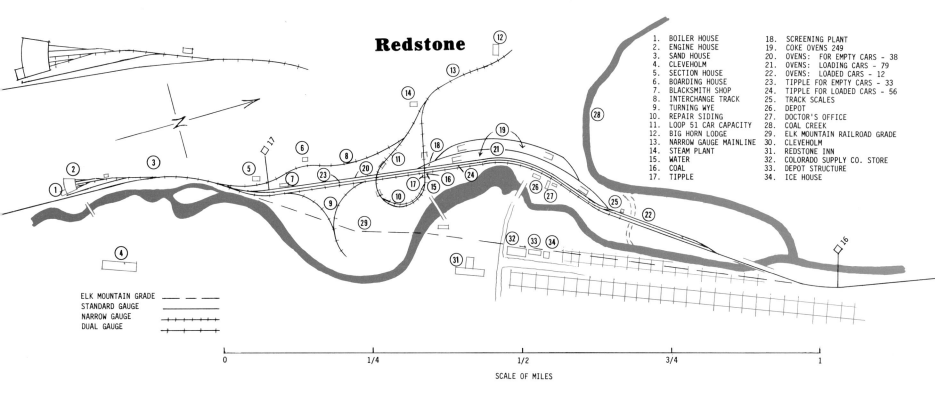

Redstone

1. BOILER HOUSE
2. ENGINE HOUSE
3. SAND HOUSE
4. CLEVEHOLM
5. SECTION HOUSE
6. BOARDING HOUSE
7. BLACKSMITH SHOP
8. INTERCHANGE TRACK
9. TURNING WYE
10. REPAIR SIDING
11. LOOP 51 CAR CAPACITY
12. BIG HORN LODGE
13. NARROW GAUGE MAINLINE
14. STEAM PLANT
15. WATER
16. COAL
17. TIPPLE
18. SCREENING PLANT
19. COKE OVENS 249
20. OVENS: FOR EMPTY CARS - 38
21. OVENS: LOADING CARS - 79
22. OVENS: LOADED CARS - 12
23. TIPPLE FOR EMPTY CARS - 33
24. TIPPLE FOR LOADED CARS - 56
25. TRACK SCALES
26. DEPOT
27. DOCTOR'S OFFICE
28. COAL CREEK
29. ELK MOUNTAIN RAILROAD GRADE
30. CLEVEHOLM
31. REDSTONE INN
32. COLORADO SUPPLY CO. STORE
33. DEPOT STRUCTURE
34. ICE HOUSE

ELK MOUNTAIN GRADE
STANDARD GAUGE
NARROW GAUGE
DUAL GAUGE

0   1/4   1/2   3/4   1

SCALE OF MILES

JOHN SMITH COLLECTION, "CAMP AND PLANT" CF&I MAGAZINE

Redstone's depot—built across the track from the coke ovens—looked like this in 1903. Dual gauge track may be seen, along with a combination passing track and siding for loaded cars of coal. The elevation of Redstone is 7,000-feet, relatively low for a Colorado mountain town.

CF&I STEEL CORP. PHOTO -- COLLECTION OF ROBERT A. LEMASSENA

Colorado & Wyoming 4-4-0 Number 103 was on loan to the Crystal River for service on the standard gauge from 1906 through 1910. This locomotive is believed to have come from the Union Pacific. Number 103 was returned to the C&W for service on passenger trains.

49

COLLECTION OF FRED AND JO MAZZULLA

JOHN C. OSGOOD . . . .

ohn Cleveland Osgood was born in Brooklyn, N. Y., on March 6, 1851. Attending school until he was 14, he then entered the business world being his sole support. From clerk to cashier at a coal camp, then cashier of a bank and then assumed control of the White Breast Coal Company. Then in 1882 the officers of the Chicago Burlington & Quincy RR. sent him to Colorado to investigate coal resources of the state. Realizing the opportunity before him, J. C. Osgood then formed the Colorado Coal Co. Mr. Osgood's executive powers were proven as the company increased and formed into C. F. & I. in 1892, from but a one-room office and a small boy as office boy.

Shortly thereafter, J. C. Osgood whipped the celebrated Chicago plunger, John W. Gates in a desperate battle for control of the C. F. & I., at the cost of some of his closest associates. He secured the investments of $40 million in coal and steel interests; then abruptly broke with C. F. & I. in 1903.

In 1893, Osgood and his first wife, Irene, an English woman, stayed at Hotel Colorado in Glenwood Springs. She was a poet and wrote romantic western short stories for magazines of the day. She was killed sometime after this by a run away horse.

After the Crystal River Railroad reached Redstone in 1900, Osgood met Alma Regina Shelgram, a Swedish girl some 20 years younger than he.

J. C. Osgood knew how miners liked to get drunk, thereby producing very little work. So his careful planning of Redstone and Coalbasin included every type of sport, dance, theatrical and club activities to keep the men's minds from drink. A special architect was hired to design the town's houses to give them the appearance of Swiss Chalet style, each one of a different design and painted in bright colors -- to more inspire the coal mine worker. The company town of the day was usually very dirty, treeless and unpainted.

When he resigned his position with C. F. & I. in 1903 – refusing to work there as a "hired hand" -- he retained ownership of the Crystal River properties. His resignation from C. F. & I. was mostly due to his great pride, partly due to the fact that he was one of the six top industrialists of that time. After devious stock manipulations, he found the company to be considered a Gould-Rockefeller enterprise, and this he could not tolerate since he had done so much to create C. F. & I.

It was during this 1900 period that his second wife, Alma, fondly known as "Lady Bountiful," shared his joys and together they chose Christmas gifts for the children of the coal camps. Osgood built Cleveholm especially for the pleasures of Lady Bountiful.

Osgood closed Cleveholm in 1913 after re-opening of the coke and coal mining that had so suddenly stopped in 1909. Many times Osgood journeyed back to his beloved Redstone seeking new ways of bringing life to the deserted village. But the times were too early for the traveler seeking a far-away homesite in the seclusion of the Crystal River valley.

In 1925, Osgood returned to Cleveholm with Lucille MacDonald as his third wife. Unfortunately, Osgood had undergone a cancer operation prior to his return and died shortly thereafter. At his request, his ashes were scattered in the valley he had so fondly loved. His bride of three years then inherited a fortune in real estate and profits of four companies.

This building photographed in 1958 still retained the original style it had been built to. Situated behind the Colorado Supply Company Store, this building may have been the first Redstone depot. The Elk Mountain Railway grade was located in the foreground and could have served the town during construction by the Crystal River Railroad.

CASEIN PAINTING BY DELL A. MCCOY

"Sunrise at Redstone"

Redstone teamed with activity during the morning hours back in "the good old days." Narrow gauge engines are shown switching the yards for the afternoon run to Coalbasin. Narrow gauge engine Number 101 chuffs by the standard gauge Number 1 as she heads down the mainline to the depot. Narrow gauge engine Number 102 shunts Ingoldsby Patent Dump Cars across the tipple trestle. Chair Mountain rises in the distance in this spring scene.

This photo, taken about **1903** at Denver Union Station, shows a group of important men of the day. From left to right: J. M. Herbert, Dr. Charles H. Corwin, the revolutionary visionary of Osgood's Minnequa Hospital, Eugene Grubb, the originator and grower of Grubbs potatoes on the Crystal River, Governor James H. Peabody, John C. Osgood, C. E. Carson and W. E. McGraw.

This workman was in the process of drawing coke from "bee-hive" ovens of the type used at Redstone. Above the oven stands a "larry" car which had a capacity of 5 to 6 tons of finely crushed coal. It had been pulled there by mule and after the load was emptied into the oven, the workmen carefully leveled it off and bricked up the doorway, leaving only a small air opening. The gasses which distilled off, ignited and burned slowly above the coal. The heat radiating downward produced coke.

THE USE OF BEE-HIVE COKE OVENS

Although some stack coke ovens were used in Colorado, the most common type was the so-called "bee-hive" oven. This name was derived from the fact that these ovens resembled dome-shaped bee-hives -- having a circular base of firebrick with a spherical dome of special-form firebrick. An opening at the top of the domes was known as the "tunnel head," or "funnel," and was used to charge the ovens, as well as to allow smoke to escape.

The fronts of these ovens had door openings approximately 3 x 3 feet, with an arch on top. After the coking process was completed, the coke was drawn out of the ovens through these doors -- out onto wharves (docks) from which the coke was loaded into railroad cars.

The backs of the ovens were either opposite each other, or else were alternated, forming a battery two deep,

SECTION THROUGH OVEN DOOR

Larry Track
Standard Gauge

Tunnel head

Earth

Pier for track support

Outside retaining wall Cut stone

Dome field brick

Oven Door →

Iron Door Frame

Door Brick

FIRE BRICK FLOOR

Ring Wall

Well tamped earth

Ring Wall should be built to bed rock

Wharf

Wharf retaining wall.

R.R. Tracks.

F.C.S.

SECTION OF TYPICAL BEE HIVE COKE OVEN.

This drawing illustrates how a bee-hive coke oven looked. The funnel at the top was 13-inches in diameter. The door opening is 3x4 feet with an arch at the top. The coke was drawn out on the wharves (docks) for loading, measuring 16 feet wide and 3 to 10 feet above the railroad track. The value of coke lies in its great crushing strength, porosity, freedom from foreign substances and the intense heat it generates while burning. These ovens have a circular base of firebrick from eleven-and-one-half-feet to thirteen-feet in diameter. An oven yields over three tons every forty-eight hours, the time required for operation.

supported by a stone retaining wall. In the space between the ovens a stone or brick pier was built, supporting "I" beams, which in turn carried rails upon which "larry" cars were run for charging the ovens. Loam was filled-in and well tamped down between the ovens, so as to retain all the heat possible. A battery of ovens consisted of from 25 to 200 or 300 on a side, as desired.

Wharves extended along the fronts of the batteries of ovens -- being two-and-one-half to three-feet lower than the bottom of the oven doors and about 16-feet wide -- allowing plenty of room for men to "pull" the ovens and for dump carts to be moved about. The height of the wharves was from three to 10-feet above the railroad tracks, depending on the type of rail cars used to transport the coke.

The coal used for coking was first processed at a "washery." There the coal was crushed, sized and conveyed to various jigs where it was washed -- that is, the coal was separated from impurities as much as possible by pulsations of water which carried the coal over slight partitions, while slate, rock and other heavier foreign matter sank down and was carried away by a conveyor. After leaving the jigs, the coal was run through revolving screens to drain off the water. It was then run through "disintegrators" where it was crushed very finely and then conveyed to "stack bins" ready to be charged into the ovens.

The stack bins were elevated so that larry cars could be run under them to be filled with five to six tons of coal. From the bins these four-wheel cars were run down tracks to the tops of the ovens -- by gravity, mules or by mechanical power. There the coal was allowed to run out through doors on the cars through the tunnel heads into the ovens. After the

charge was in the ovens, they were leveled by means of a scraper through the door at the front of each oven. The doors were then bricked up and sealed, with the exception of a small hole at the top to admit air. The gasses which were generated, ignited and burned slowly downward, producing coke.

At the end of some 48-hours, the doors were taken down and the coke was carefully watered down to put out the fire. After quenching the fire, the ovens were allowed to stand for a few minutes to steam off -- when the coke was then ready to "pull." This was done largely by hand by means of a "ravel," or scraper. From the wharves the coke was forked into railroad cars -- pitch-forks being used to remove ashes and unusable fine coke.

The coal screening plant at Redstone looked like this photo shown looking north about 1902. The Crystal River Railroad ran between the "bents" (upright-timbers) beneath this structure. Gondolas were loaded under the coal bin, and the locomotives were fueled and watered here.

The Colorado Supply Company store was the largest building in Redstone in this view of 1902.

J. B. Bowen, Manager
Number 24 Redstone.

The Colorado Supply Company stores issued script and took it in trade for merchandise in the coal camps. The denominations were 5 cents, 10 cents, 25 cents, 50 cents, $1.00, $2.00 and $5.00.

The end was near for the Redstone coal and coke plant when this photo was taken in the spring of 1909. The Coalbasin mine had shut down in January of that year, thereby bringing an end to the coke-oven operation. The Crystal River Railroad continued operations until December 8, 1910, when the Crystal River & San Juan began running trains through to Carbondale. To the left may be seen the two rows of coke ovens, which numbered 200. The depot sits on the curve between the ovens and the bridge. The bin to the left of the trestle housed a washery unit on the roof that cleaned and crushed the coal which was then stored in the bins. Note the dual gauge track that runs over the trestle so that coal, from Placita on the standard gauge, could be processed.

57

Photographed in 1901, Redstone was in full production with the coke ovens burning. The box cars were used to haul the coke and one gondola of coal can be seen spotted on the middle track, having been loaded under the trestle. Chair Mountain rises in the misty background to the south. Two Patent Ingoldsby dump cars have just discharged their loads into the bin on the trestle. These cars brought the run-of-mine coal from Coalbasin down the narrow gauge. Coal tonnage ranged from 15,000 to 25,000 tons a month. Coke tonnage handled amounted to 6,000 to 11,000 tons per month. Combined, this total is about one-half of the present day haulage.

This view, taken in 1900, faces toward the south and shows the Redstone depot beside the coke ovens. To the right of the ovens may be seen the foundation of the second row -- under construction at the time. The ramshackle shanty town where Redstone's first residents lived was located beside these ovens. On the trestle, more than 15 Ingoldsby Patent dump cars, loaded with coal from the Coalbasin mine, are in the process of dumping their loads.

In 1901, the Redstone roundhouse housed all four iron ponies of the Crystal River Railroad. The stall on the far left was used to interchange standard and narrow gauge trucks under the rotary snow plow. A gondola loaded with coal was spotted for the boiler house behind the roundhouse. The Crystal River Railroad's mainline to Placita is to the left of this view. The cottage to the right was the residence of J. C. Osgood's gamekeeper, who was responsible for the game reserve on the hillside back of this building.

Roy Coombs, a small boy in this photo taken in 1903, posed aboard the largest of the CR narrow gauge locomotives. Number 103 was purchased from the Baldwin Locomotive Works and arrived on the Crystal River, April 18, 1903. This heavier outside-frame 2-8-0 allowed the railroad to increase their coal tonnage from Coalbasin because the 103 was rated to haul 10 empties upgrade whereas the 101 and 102 could pull only seven empties each. Link and pin couplings were used on the narrow gauge line until its end in 1909. At a later date, Roy Coombs worked on the CR&SJ as a fireman.

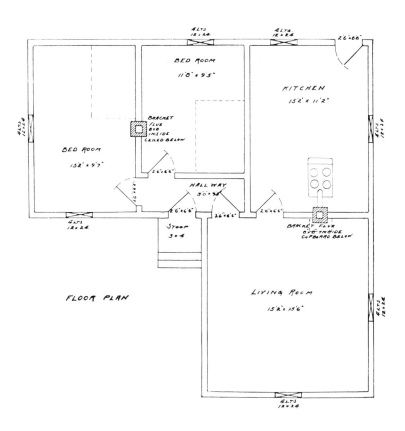

FLOOR PLAN

One floor plan of houses built by the company for employees is shown here. This was in the good old days before indoor plumbing was common. Today these homes are used as summer cottages in Redstone. In 1901, families could rent a five-room cottage for $18.50 a month.

The more expensive homes in Redstone were built up the hillside and were originally used by superintendents and other company officials. Looking north, Mount Sopris rises in the distance. Even today, Redstone is one of the most pleasant villages in Colorado.

These crude log cabins were constructed by miners at Old Redstone, located on the west side of the Crystal River. J. C. Osgood made several attempts to get this side of town to clean up. Eventually these residents moved into new company houses.

The Redstone Inn in 1952 was much smaller than it is today. This hostelry was built by CF&I for the bachelor workmen in 1901. Meals were shared in a large dining room and the entire building was constructed with the finest woodwork of the day, featuring large stone fireplaces and hunting trophies adorning the walls.

PHOTO BY MORRISON A. SMITH   COLLECTION OF JOHN W. MAXWELL

Big Horn Lodge was built on the west side of the Crystal River, on the hillside overlooking the town of Redstone. Designed as a meeting place for the CF&I board of directors, the lodge was seldom used because the smoke and fumes from the coke ovens in the valley were an annoyance if the wind was not right. Special sterling silver flatware bearing the Big Horn crest in filigree, along with the finest linens, decorated the tables. This building also housed a game room equipped with a bowling alley.

PHOTO BY L. C. MC CLURE   COLLECTION OF GEORGE AND DOROTHY WHITE

63

On stage in the Redstone Clubhouse, the Redstone Band proudly poses with their instruments donated by J. C. Osgood. The instruments were the finest money could buy, being triple-silver-plated. The professor of music, Eliseo Jacoe, had the trying time of holding together a large enough number to make good music, due to the fast turnover of workers employed by the railroad and CF&I.

The auditorium on the second floor of the Redstone Club was built for the entertainment of camp workers. The main floor included a billiard and pool room, a library and reading room, a shower and a bar. The bar adopted the rule that each man could buy a drink only for himself, thereby cutting down on drunkenness that would happen so often when men would begin treating one another.

This view shows the Redstone Fire House on the hillside above town in 1963. A small hand-pumper was used by the volunteer fire department. In the early 1900's the Redstone band practiced here on the second floor.

The Redstone Public School was ornately built of redstone and brick, topped off with a bell tower. This building stood next to the club house. The fire house was located across the street.

The castle named Cleveholm by J. C. Osgood cost about $500,000 to build in 1903. It was approached from gate houses at either side and had a large stable at the north approach where the harnesses were kept in glass-domed cases. Built in an era when financial success was reflected in material display, the floors were covered with oriental rugs, woodwork was solid mahogany, there were vast fireplaces bearing the Osgood crest, many halls and rooms had domes covered in gold leaf with leather covering the library walls. Silver goblets, serving trays and centerpieces were kept in hand-carved cabinets with curved plate glass.

Entrance was made to the Cleveholm estate through this European-style gate over the cobblestone drive. A tug on the bell cord would announce one's arrival.

J. C. Osgood proudly offers his second wife, Alma, a helping hand. The fellow in the center is probably T. M. Gibb, Osgood's right hand man at Redstone during this 1903 view. J. C. Osgood's second wife was fondly referred to as "Lady Bountiful". She was especially well-remembered by the children of Redstone and Coalbasin for her generosity during Christmas seasons when the Osgoods would have a grand ball where each boy and girl would be given an expensive gift.

The Cleveholm drawing room was designed so that "Lady Bountiful" could look through her bedroom window on the second floor to see the arrival of guests. The chandeliers are inlaid with gold and the wallpaper is hand-made. The Osgood crest is built into the red sandstone fireplace.

The game room at Cleveholm on the lower floor was adorned with hunting trophies and old rifles and muskets. A wine closet was built beneath the pool cues.

The Cleveholm library had green leather wallpaper, hand-tooled with gold.
The far side of this room had a fireplace made of green onyx and the ceiling
is covered in gold leaf.

Looking to the east in this view taken about 1908, Redstone is barely visible in the trees.   The narrow gauge branch to Coalbasin is in the foreground with the town barn behind this.   The coke oven rows stretch through the valley.   Beyond this, the Elk Mountain Lodge may be seen to the right.   Higher on the hillside, the large buildings left to right are: The school and clubhouse with the firehouse in between.

COLLECTION OF ROBERT SEWELL

This view of the big narrow gauge Number 103, taken in 1903, was probably at the scene of a snow slide. The coal tender is in a tipsy condition and company officials are pondering over the mishap. This was on the interchange track at Redstone.

A depot waiting room.

Crystal River Railroad "High Line"

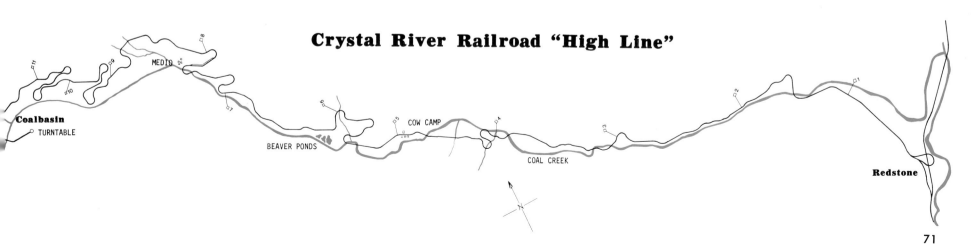

PHOTO BY RICHARD KINDIG

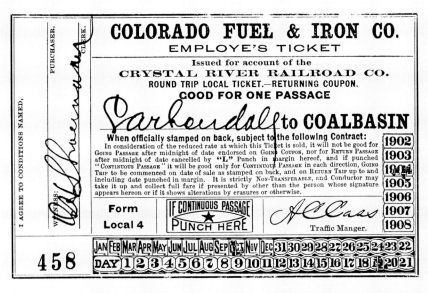

Photographed at Montrose, Colorado, on August 23, 1940, D&RGW Number 360 is shown waiting for orders. This was originally Crystal River Railroad Number 101, built by Baldwin in 1899. She was scrapped in 1950.

October 19, 1904 was the date punched on this Employees Ticket. These tickets were issued to workmen of the coal camps at a reduced price. This encouraged the employee to take advantage of the best mode of travel and assured the company that the ticket holder would show up for work.

COLLECTION OF MORRIS ABBOTT

PHOTO BY RICHARD KINDIG

Photographed at Cimarron, Colorado, on June 6, 1940, D&RGW Number 361 simmers in the hot sun. This was originally Crystal River Railraod Number 102, built by Baldwin in 1899. On the Rio Grande, she and her sister engine, Number 360, were Class C-21. She was scrapped in 1951.

The Crystal River narrow gauge 2-8-0 Number 102 was brand new -- just out of the Baldwin works -- when this photo was taken in 1899. When the line ceased all operations in 1914, she was taken to Pueblo, sold to the D&RG in 1916, and served the Rio Grande until 1951, along with Number 101. Both were then scrapped. These were the first outside-frame engines owned by the D&RG. They were often called, "Little Mudhens" by crewmen.

COLLECTION OF H. L. BROADBELT

In the color view above, the D&RGW had ex-Crystal River Number 103 in the engine terminal at Durango, Colorado, on June 4, 1940. Notice the double-lung pump mounted on the side, the new "cow catcher," the incandesant headlight, new tender, a smaller cab, and a shotgun stack. The smokebox has been shortened about 18-inches. She was scrapped in 1949.

Taken at Salida, Colorado, in 1924, this photo shows D&RGW Number 375 (former CR Number 103) shortly after being renumbered from 432. She still sports the cab built by the Crystal River -- enormous for a narrow gauge engine.

A story was told by Gilbert Lathrop about this engine when it arrived on the Rio Grande. The firemen could not get her to steam properly no matter what technique was tried. One day Gilbert

was called to fire the 432 for his dad (a D&RG engineer). He had the same trouble with the fire that the other men had until finally in disgust, Gilbert just dropped the coal in the firebox instead of spreading it over the fire evenly. Suddenly the safety valves opened with a roar and from then on the needle on the steam gauge stayed at 160 pounds. This unconventional firing was burning her up! According to Gilbert Lathrop, this proved to be the best-running engine on the D&RGW at that time.

DELL A. MCCOY

Shown above is one of the diesel trucks currently used to haul coal from the Coalbasin washing plant to the storage tipple at Carbondale. These trucks carry 27.5 tons of coal per trip, or approximately the same tonnage carried by the Ingoldby railroad cars. This is about half the capacity of each of the modern hopper cars used to haul the coal over the D&RGW to Geneva, Utah.

Approaching Milepost 2, engine Number 101 pulls about six empty Ingoldsby dump cars upgrade on a late afternoon extra. The rocky canyon is quite red at this point, giving credence to the name, "Redstone", which is in the valley below. Coal Creek tumbles through the chasm to the right.

A narrow gauge locomotive bound for Coalbasin chuffs steadily upgrade along the hillside with a string of empties for the mine. Far below in the valley are several beaver ponds surrounded by vast groves of aspen. The West Elk Mountains add grandeur to the scene — with their hillsides covered with autumn colors.

COLLECTION OF FRED AND JO MAZZULLA

CASEIN PAINTING BY DELL A. MCCOY

"Upgrade Coalbasin Freight"

Bridge B3 was one of the timber structures placed on the Coalbasin branch that had been removed from the Aspen & Western grade. This view is near the four-mile post.

The "merry-go-round" on the Crystal River Railroad looked like this at Milepost 4. The trestle was Bridge 4 and today the Mid-Continent Coal & Coke Company uses this site for their coal-washing and screening plant. The color photo on the next page shows this plant as it looked during the autumn of 1971.

Posed in the lower canyon just above Redstone, a Crystal River narrow gauge train is shown here with a new Ingoldsby dump car in 1900.

Coal Washing plant of the Mid Continent Coal & Coke Co. -- formerly on the Coalbasin Branch.

PHOTO BY DAVID S. DIGERNESS

The Coalbasin Branch is shown above, under construction sometime before 1899. At this point the grade climbs high above the river, and loops back and forth into Medio. This railroad was laid without tieplates and had only dirt ballast.

A so-called "Zig-Zag" on the Crystal River Railroad between Redstone and Coalbasin was located at mileposts 5 and 6. A cow camp was located here, just to the right of the lower level of the grade.

Bridge E4 on the Coalbasin branch was an impressive structure near milepost 5. This was located just below the cow camp. This bridge was made of wood timbers with steel rod vertical braces.

When photographed in 1971, Milepost 8 was still making its lonely stand among the quaking aspens, along the grade of Coalbasin Branch of the Crystal River Railroad, 62 years after abandonment of the line. The ties and ballast have long since dissappeared.

A leased D&RG 2-8-0, Number 30 shown here pushing two flat cars carrying track layers -- was used on the Coalbasin Branch early in 1900 to lay rail. This scene is at Bridge A5, just above the cow camp, five-and-one-half miles from Redstone. Track laying was completed on November 22, 1900. The Crystal River engines may have been enroute from Pueblo at this time, since they were delivered new, to CF&I, from Baldwin late in 1900.

COLLECTION OF CHAS. C. SQUIRES

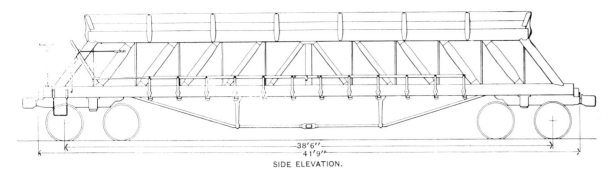

SIDE ELEVATION.

38'6"
41'9"

THE INGOLDSBY AUTOMATIC CAR CO.'S PATENT OPEN DUMP CAR.
WOOD CONSTRUCTION.

THE CAR HERE SHOWN HAS A REMOVABLE 16 INCH FALSE TOP, AND WHEN THE LOAD IS CROWNED TO 30 DEGREE HEAP, IT HOLDS
105,000 POUNDS OF COAL.

LOADED WITH REGULAR SERVICE LOAD OF 110,000 POUNDS OF ANY MATERIAL, THE
RATIO OF DEAD WEIGHT TO PAYING FREIGHT IS ABOUT
38 PER CENT.

THE CUBIC CONTENTS OF THIS CAR WHEN LOAD IS CROWNED TO A 30 DEGREE HEAP IS
2,022 CUBIC FEET.

On the bottom view is shown the strong center member, which takes the direct strain resulting from the impact of head-on collisions or rough coupling, and also the diagonal struts and V tie rods, which tend to distribute this strain over the entire floor system.

The truss rods shown on the elevation are large U bolts resting on cast iron saddles directly over the bolsters, and being fastened together by the turn buckles at the center of the car.

One-half of the total load is carried by the center member of the car, while each Howe truss side carries one-quarter of the load.

As shown on the TOP VIEW, the doors can be opened one at a time or altogether, as desired.

For CROSS SECTIONS of this car in various positions see pages 72 and 73.

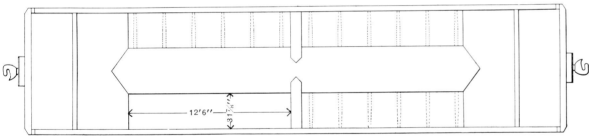

12'6"
31⅞"

TOP VIEW, SHOWING ONLY ONE DOOR OPEN.

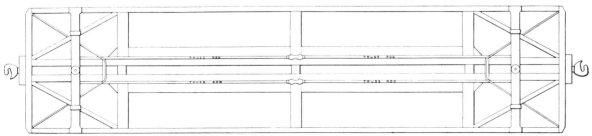

BOTTOM VIEW, SHOWING FLOOR SYSTEM.

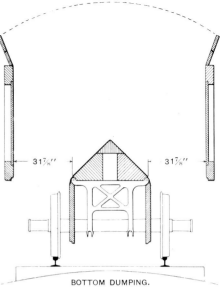

31⅞"   31⅞"

BOTTOM DUMPING.
VERTICAL DROP THROUGH OPENING OF 133 SQ. FT.

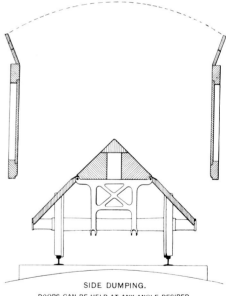

SIDE DUMPING.
DOORS CAN BE HELD AT ANY ANGLE DESIRED.

73

PHOTO BY RUSS COLLMAN

The Ingoldsby patent dump car was designed in such a way that an entire car could be unloaded in seconds at the pull of a lever. This unloading could also be accomplished at speeds of over 40 miles per hour without fouling the train. Usually cars were made so that it was necessary to shovel the load out by hand, and the more expensive drop bottom hoppers would not entirely unload without some hand work. Ingoldsby especially demonstrated the versatility of their car in the winter of 1900 with frozen loads of coal out of Coalbasin. Eight cars were dumped in but ten minutes

at the Redstone tipple. Sometimes the snow would mix with the coal and freeze the entire load, but a few pokes with a bar would loosen the entire mass. The Crystal River Railroad purchased forty of these cars.

The abandoned grade of the Coalbasin Branch could still be plainly seen during the summer of 1960 on this curve above Milepost 7. The splendor of the changing scenes one encounters at different elevations makes this one of the most enjoyable hikes one can take in Colorado.

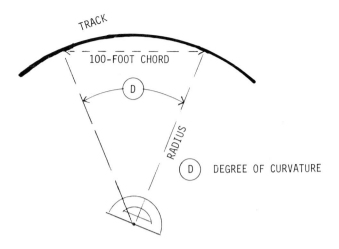

The degree of curvature is found by stretching a cord 100-ft. between two points on the center line of track. The amount the track turns in this distance is the degree of curvature.

One of the prized possessions of the Colorado Railroad Museum is this Crystal River Railroad milepost. Robert Richardson, curator of the museum, found Milepost R-11 at the edge of Coalbasin several years ago. Needless to say, he brought it back with him -- eventually placing it along the museum's three-foot gauge track at Golden, Colorado. The builder's number plate is off of engine Number 103, the lines largest narrow gauge locomotive. The link on the side of the post was picked up along the right-of-way many years after the line was abandoned.

PHOTO BY DELL A. MC COY

Narrow gauge engine Number 101 heads for Coalbasin, working as a helper. She was on the tail end of a train of Ingoldsby dump cars and cars loaded with merchandise.

While hiking along the old grade of the Coalbasin Branch during the fall of 1971, the photographer captured this color view of a ridge of the Huntsman Hills. Coalbasin is located along this ridge, approximately three miles beyond the point where this photo was taken.

On the narrow gauge "High Line" branch of the Crystal River Railroad one may look back toward Redstone and take in this view near Milepost 9 at the base of the hillside to the track in the foreground.

In this rare view, rotary snow plow Number AB2 is being readied for a trip down the High Line to open up the snowed-in track. This rotary plow was sold to the D&RG about 1916 and was re-numbered "00". It was used on the narrow gauge lines in southwestern Colorado.

On February 18, 1903, miners were called out to shovel through a snowslide on the High Line near Coalbasin. The avalanche covered the track to a depth of 20-feet, making the rotary plow useless. If the line were snowed in for any length of time, the camp would run out of provisions. With day-time temperatures reaching no more than 20 degrees below zero (F.), this type of work taxed the miner's constitutions to the utmost.

A Crystal River Railroad narrow gauge train heads for Coalbasin with empties on a cold winter day. This was probably the morning train, which would stop at Medio on the way down to Redstone, allowing the upgrade mixed train to pass. The engine is either Number 101 or Number 102, photographed in action -- a very difficult feat during this period of time.

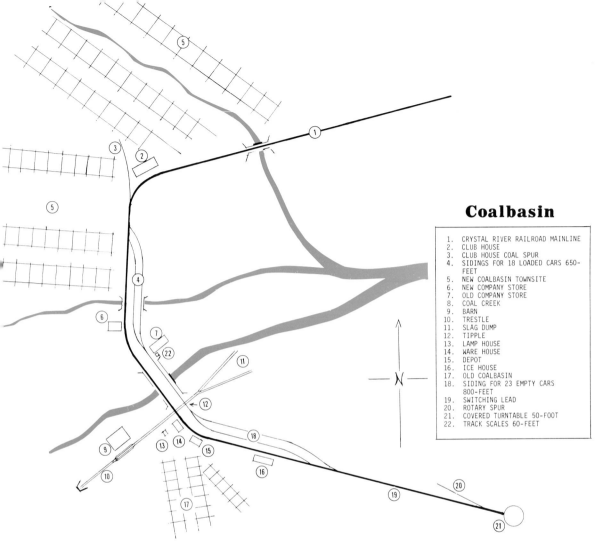

Coalbasin

1. CRYSTAL RIVER RAILROAD MAINLINE
2. CLUB HOUSE
3. CLUB HOUSE COAL SPUR
4. SIDINGS FOR 18 LOADED CARS 650-FEET
5. NEW COALBASIN TOWNSITE
6. NEW COMPANY STORE
7. OLD COMPANY STORE
8. COAL CREEK
9. BARN
10. TRESTLE
11. SLAG DUMP
12. TIPPLE
13. LAMP HOUSE
14. WARE HOUSE
15. DEPOT
16. ICE HOUSE
17. OLD COALBASIN
18. SIDING FOR 23 EMPTY CARS 800-FEET
19. SWITCHING LEAD
20. ROTARY SPUR
21. COVERED TURNTABLE 50-FOOT
22. TRACK SCALES 60-FEET

JOHN SMITH COLLECTION "CAMP AND PLANT" CF&I MAGAZINE

This was the miner's favorite day at Coalbasin -- payday. The group is waiting for the pay car to arrive at the Coalbasin depot during March of 1903. The miners were given brass checks to attach to the pit car they loaded with coal. Once the pit car was weighed on tipple scale the weigh boss would record this on the daily bulletin with the number attached on the brass check. This depot was 9,443-feet above sea level. (It might be noted that the young boys in this picture were not employees.)

The joy of the hard-working miners was the Coalbasin Club, located next to the track as this 1902 view shows. The club had four main rooms, a front veranda and a basement. Immediately to the rear of the veranda was a bar-room being plain as possible without mirrors to render it attractive and without any display of bottled goods or other means of advertisement or suggestion to drink. To the right is the billiard and pool room. The first room to the left is the card and game room, while on the extreme left is the reading room, equipped with magazines and periodicals. Women and children could not enter the club except by permission of the board of directors. The "no treating rule" was enforced here and the men considered it "bad form" to become intoxicated. However, on the fourth of July eight barrels of beer, four kegs of whiskey and a large amount of wine were brought in by train for a "big blowout". Work in the mine was halted for several days.

JOHN SMITH COLLECTION "CAMP AND PLANT" CF&I MAGAZINE

The original Store Number 26 of the Colorado Supply Company first opened for business at Coalbasin in August of 1900. It is shown in the lower photograph. During the following year, the store was moved across the track into the building shown in the upper view. Although the second store was constructed on a beautiful location, it later proved to be an unwise choice for a building site. One winter -- not too long before the Coalbasin camp was closed -- a severe snowslide came roaring down the precipitous slope behind the store, knocking the building off its foundation and over the tracks. When the avalanche hit, the store manager was asleep in the loft. Before he knew what hit him, he had been picked up and deposited in the midst of the store wreckage down the hillside.

COLLECTION OF JOHN SMITH "CAMP AND PLANT" CF&I MAGAZINE

L. A. Hanawald Manager
Number 26, Coalbasin.

CF&I MAGAZINE "CAMP AND PLANT" --
WESTERN COLLECTION, DENVER PUBLIC LIBRARY

This panoramic photo of Coalbasin was taken in the spring of 1901, before the second company store was built. At this time, the large building in the center was the store. Construction was still underway on the trestle leading to the tipple. Coal-loading was already in process. Empty Ingoldsby dump cars can be seen on the grade above the trestle and the loaded cars have been spotted below the store. Pit cars were run out on the trestle where they dumped loads of mine slag on the dump pile behind the store. An ice house sits behind the empty cars while the railroad depot is the building just beyond the trestle. "Old Coalbasin" was the group of houses on the distant hillside.

This view of Coalbasin was taken c. 1904. It shows the new Colorado Supply Company store which was built across the track from the old store. The covered turntable can be faintly seen to the far left. The Club House is in the cluster of houses near the center, next to three car loads of coal. By 1902, 265 men were employed at Coalbasin. They were Austrians, Italians and Slavs, as well as native-born Americans. Today's mine operates over the ridge and a new tunnel has been opened above the old one in the saddle of Capital Peak shown in this photograph. Today, only one lonely log building remains out of all the buildings once at Coalbasin. It was used by the miners to store their lamps. It stands near the ruins of the tipple.

The proud engineer and fireman of Crystal River narrow gauge engine Number 102 lean against their polished iron pony at the Coalbasin tipple. When this photograph was taken (c. 1901), the carbon-arc headlight was a new innovation and the capped stack was in vogue. Engineers of this period had the dangerous job of handling braking with straight air brakes on the Coalbasin Branch's 4.4-percent downgrade -- with several-hundred tons of coal in tow. The Ingoldsby dump-car -- to the left of the engine -- is being loaded with run-of-mine coal. These cars were rolled downgrade from the storage yard by gravity for loading. Brakemen controlled them by working hand-brakes as they drifted under the tipple.

This photo was published September 13, 1902, showing the trestle leading from the portal of the mine tunnel to the tipple at Coalbasin. The trestle was 50 feet high at this point and ten loaded pit cars are shown descending. This trestle was 1,400-feet in length. Later, 20 pit cars per trip doubled the mine output. Horses were used in the depths of the mine to move the pit cars. Records show that CF&I owned the mine while J. C. Osgood had full control of the railroad.

The "Rocky Mountain canary" pictured here was the most important pack animal in its time. Sometimes a train of 100 of these sure-footed animals hauled in machinery and supplies to the camps around timberline and higher. Any man that headed a train of these critters soon knew more musical swear words than he knew regular words.

Copyright 1902, by Herman Nash

93

Rotary snow plow Number AB2 rests on the special spur laid for it at the end of the Coalbasin Branch. The turntable was inside a covered building to ward off the heavy snowfall of the altitude of nearly 10,000 feet. This view looks to the east and the "High Line" had worked its way up from the valley, almost 2,000 feet below.

The track shown leading to the turntable allowed up-grade trains to pull their loads past the plow and switch the empties off to the holding yard just back of the photographer. The rotary snowplow was used on both standard gauge and narrow gauge lines of the Crystal River Railroad.

"Camp and Plant" magazine called this the "Meanderings of the High Line or narrow gauge branch of the Crystal River Railroad". This is indeed a good description of the contortions the Coalbasin Branch of the Crystal River Railroad went through. This view was taken from the covered turntable at Coalbasin. The curves were 40-degrees and the grade was 4.5% between the loops. Degree of curvature is figured by stretching a cord 100 feet long between two points on the center line of track. The amount the track turns in this distance is the degree of curvature. One loop below Coalbasin was 50-degrees.

The Ingoldsby patent dump cars were given a severe weather test at Coalbasin during the winter of 1900. The view at upper right shows train of empties which had just arrived from Redstone. The crews on engines 101 and 102 are busily plowing out the mainline with flanger Number B1. The engine in the far distance is near the turntable.

Here the crew had coupled rotary snowplow Number AB2 onto the front of the train, with engines 101 and 102, way cars 01 and 02 and flanger B1 following. The way cars were used as the conductor's offices and shelter for the train crews. The flanger was tacked on the rear to clear snow in case the train must back up. The train is on the mainline at Coalbasin, having passed under the coal tipple.

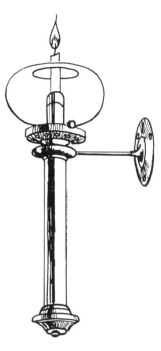

This pen and ink drawing by Dell A. McCoy was drawn from the actual brass lamp that decorated the Coalbasin Club.

The remains of the Coalbasin turntable pit looked like this during the fall of 1962. The town limits were on the far hillside, and the railroad came up from Redstone on the right and circled around the basin to reach the turntable. The railroad was nearly twelve miles in length at this point.

During the last week of September in 1971, the Crystal River was flanked by the beautiful changing colors of a cool, crisp Colorado autumn. Chair Mountain rises in the distance to the south while the highway that was originally the Crystal River Railroad may be seen in the background. The Crystal River Ranch that J. C. Osgood built is on the left bank of the river at this point. His railroad siding was located at the bridge to the ranch, and was used for spotting his private car, "Sunrise," and a diner.

COLLECTION OF JOHN T. HERMAN

COLLECTION OF THE LATE WILLIAM MC MANUS

Photographed during the winter of 1942, after a fresh snowfall, the railroad dismantling train is shown working downgrade near Hays Creek on the CR&SJ. Engine Number 1 has box car Number 101 in tow along with a flat car equipped with winch and cable to draw the rail onto the following flat cars. This box car was the oldest piece of rolling stock on the line, having arrived new in 1900 for use on the narrow gauge branch of the Crystal River Railroad.

Leased Colorado & Wyoming Railroad 4-6-0 Number 701 trundles downgrade at Hays Creek as the Crystal River thunders alongside the track in this narrow part of the canyon. This scene was photographed during the busy years of the marble trade (c. 1912), as may be seen by the flat car loads of marble.

This 1942 winter scene shows Morse Brothers Machinery Company pulling out the rails of the CR&SJ at Hays Creek. The rail was being winched up over the metal plate and loaded onto the flat cars. Engine Number 1 is on the head end with box car 101 following. Hays Falls cascades down through a gorge to the left.

COLLECTION OF BILL SMITH

Chair Mountain rises against a cloud-covered sky in the spring of 1950. An unmeasurable wealth is contained in the snows that flank her arms. Peaks such as this provide a continuous flow of water throughout the year for the Crystal River. In this view the river is flowing beside the roadway that was previously the grade of the CR&SJ. The original wagon road to Marble and Crystal City skirts the railroad grade higher up on the hillside. This is near the narrows of the Canyon, with Hays Creek just out of sight, around the hill in the foreground.

PHOTO BY THE LATE JOHN B. SCHUTTE

JOHN SMITH COLLECTION CAMP AND PLANT -- CF&I MAGAZINE "CAMP AND PLANT"

COLLECTION OF JOHN SMITH   CF&I "CAMP AND PLANT" MAGAZINE

The Crystal River Railroad surgeon, Dr. Taylor, makes an imposing picture astride his mount at Placita in 1901. The Placita depot may be seen in the background, having just been built. The station siding had not yet been laid at this time.

In the 1900's, a CF&I company store was built by the Colorado Supply Company at Placita, officially called, Store Number 20. This was a simple structure compared with the ones at Coalbasin and Redstone.

PHOTO BY RUSS COLLMAN

This springtime waterfall cascades into the Crystal River from the water of Hays Creek. Often one may see deer and elk feeding along the banks here.

This impressive photo was taken on November 11, 1941, after the ICC had granted abandonment during September of the same year. Apparently the marble business was too brisk to permit the end of operations at this time, and Morse Brothers Machinery Company of Denver was forced to postpone salvage operations until winter. Pictured just north of Placita, the CR&SJ needed extra steam to climb up from the station and continue the journey downgrade to Carbondale. Chair Mountain towers in the background with a new layer of fresh fallen snow. The coal tipple may be seen to the left of coach Number 9. Notice that the grade has been rip-rapped with marble slabs, waste material from the dump at the Yule Marble Co. mill.

PHOTO BY MORRISON A. SMITH
COLLECTION OF JOHN W. MAXWELL

This was the original Placita coal mine opening on the Crystal River Railroad about four miles south of Redstone. The line was being relocated at this point; a deep cut had been blasted out to straighten the mainline. In this view the photographer is looking south and was taken in 1909. A siding with a capacity for six cars ran along the hillside here for coal loading.

Built Up Iron Pilot.

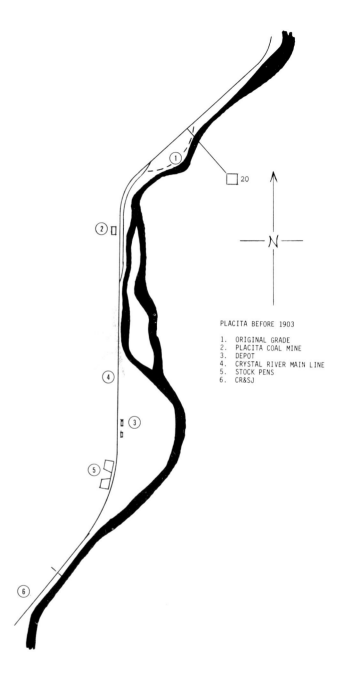

PLACITA BEFORE 1903

1. ORIGINAL GRADE
2. PLACITA COAL MINE
3. DEPOT
4. CRYSTAL RIVER MAIN LINE
5. STOCK PENS
6. CR&SJ

Names of Parts of Fig. 740.

1 Engine Frame
3 Pilot Brace
4 Pilot or Bumper Beam
11 Coupler Pocket
32 Front Platform Plate

Fig. 740—Built-up Iron Pilot. Baldwin Locomotive Works.

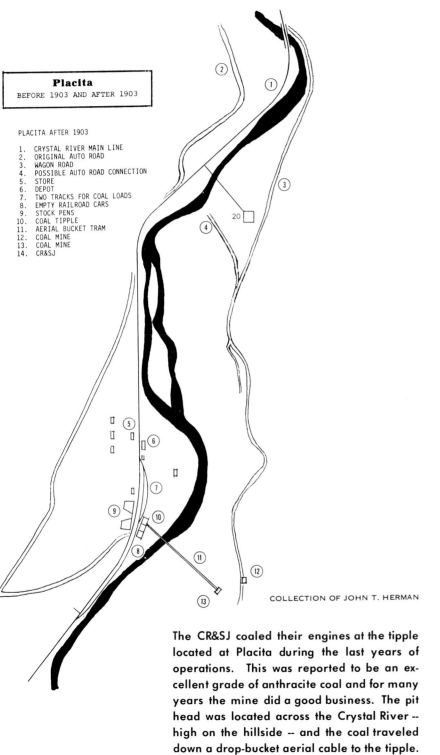

Placita
BEFORE 1903 AND AFTER 1903

PLACITA AFTER 1903

1. CRYSTAL RIVER MAIN LINE
2. ORIGINAL AUTO ROAD
3. WAGON ROAD
4. POSSIBLE AUTO ROAD CONNECTION
5. STORE
6. DEPOT
7. TWO TRACKS FOR COAL LOADS
8. EMPTY RAILROAD CARS
9. STOCK PENS
10. COAL TIPPLE
11. AERIAL BUCKET TRAM
12. COAL MINE
13. COAL MINE
14. CR&SJ

COLLECTION OF JOHN T. HERMAN

The CR&SJ coaled their engines at the tipple located at Placita during the last years of operations. This was reported to be an excellent grade of anthracite coal and for many years the mine did a good business. The pit head was located across the Crystal River -- high on the hillside -- and the coal traveled down a drop-bucket aerial cable to the tipple.

In this photograph, the dismantling train had stopped in Placita during the winter of 1942. The abandoned coal tipple stands to the left while, to the right, are stock pens that were very much in use during the last years of operation, making it necessary to operate both Number 1 and Number 2 simultaneously during the stock movements.

Placita (meaning "little place" in Spanish) was photographed in 1911 by D&RG photographer, George Beam. This was at the end of Crystal River Railroad trackage. The Crystal River & San Juan connected just over the hill in the foreground. The surrounding river bottom-lands are sage-covered and dotted with scrub oak, spruce, willows and cottonwoods. On the higher slopes, verdant aspen forests predominate. Notice the wiggly track of the main-line and the crude stock pen, largely hidden by sagebrush.

With the throttle open, Cookman Chidester makes a run for the 3-percent grade to Camp Genter. The Placita coal mine pit head may be seen across the river, a short distance up the hillside to the right. Along this stretch of track, the beaver were constantly attempting to dam the Crystal River, often nearly inundating the roadbed in the process. A train of this length was about maximum upgrade tonnage that the CR&SJ's Number 2 could handle. Photographed on September 6, 1941.

CRYSTAL RIVER & SAN JUAN

PLACITA

CRYSTAL RIVER RAILROAD

CRYSTAL RIVER & SAN JUAN

OLD McCLURE PASS ROAD

McCLURE

PITKIN COUNTY
GUNNISON COUNTY

CRYSTAL RIVER & SAN JUAN

CHAIR CREEK

LILY LAKE

CAMP GENTER

PROSPECT

C. R. & S. J. Ry. before 1910

RAPID CREEK

HOLLANDS

FORTCH'S

Marble

MILTON CREEK

RASPBERRY CREEK

I ncorporated on October 24, 1906, the standard gauge Crystal River & San Juan ran their first train on November 23, 1906. The line was constructed from a connection with the Crystal River Railroad at Placita, Colorado, and ran from there in a southerly direction 7.3-miles to Marble, Colorado. The purpose of this railroad was to ship finished marble out, and to haul supplies and equipment into Marble.

After December 8, 1910, a lease was made with the Crystal River Railroad for the use of their right-of-way so that the Crystal River & San Juan could run on into Carbondale. The Colorado Fuel & Iron Company had decided it no longer needed coal and coke from Coalbasin -- removing the primary reason for the existence of the Crystal River Railroad. This created an awkward situation for both the CR&SJ and the CRR, which culminated in the leasing of the CRR to the CR&SJ in 1910. In effect, this permitted the CR&SJ to operate both railroads, giving the combined line a total of 29.4-miles of trackage.

During the period from 1906 to approximately 1910, the CR&SJ and the CRR interchanged freight and passengers at Redstone. The CR&SJ would run two short trains each day and sometimes extras on Sundays. Operations at the Marble finishing plant were shut down after April 15, 1917, due to depression in the construction industry. Operations resumed on April 5, 1922, after the company re-organized.

0   1/4   1/2   1   2

SCALE OF MILES

September 30, 1917, was the date the CR&SJ temporarily ceased operations -- while the marble works were closed. A new lease was then drawn up with the Crystal River Railroad, December 1, 1919, when all operations halted on that line due to the lack of coking business. July 24, 1924, the marble holdings were merged into one company, named Colorado Consolidated Yule Marble Company, with offices at Marble, Colorado.

The marble holdings which Col. Channing Meek purchased in 1905 -- with the intention of beginning stone quarrying and finishing operations on a grand scale was named Colorado-Yule Marble Company and they were purchased from the Colorado Midland Railroad, who in turn had purchased them from W. D. Parry and Partners. The greatest amount of business at Marble was conducted during this period, until shortly after Col. Meek's death during the winter of 1912. At this time, some 3,000 persons lived and carried on their work in and around Marble.

At the beginning of railroad operations, engine Number 6, a small 2-6-0, was used to haul freight and passengers over this standard gauge road. On December 8, 1910, Colorado & Wyoming Railroad engine Number 701, a 4-6-0, was run from Carbondale to Marble and used as a sister engine with Number 6. The 701 was leased from the C&W, probably at a very reasonable rate since the Crystal River Railroad wanted out of the railroad game at this time. The CR&SJ was on the spot with but one engine to continue business, and the Crystal River Railroad had not yet obtained official abandonment authorization for their railroad. The CR&SJ conductor's book shows the 701 as

being used regularly on the run from Marble to Carbondale. The turntable pit had been completed just prior to this on December 17, 1909.

Records show that on October 18, 1910, the 6-spot engine and train Number 22 left Marble before sunrise -- at 5:00 a.m. -- with two loads of marble and one car of merchandise, arriving at Redstone at 5:55 a.m. The Crystal River Railroad caboose Number 2 was already cut off at the depot and Number 6 then coupled onto a load of Colorado Midland coal and the CR&SJ caboose Number 01 (painted red). Train Number 23 then departed for Marble, arriving there at 7:05 a.m. After lunch train Number 24 left Marble at 12:20 p.m. arriving at Redstone with CR&SJ caboose 01 and 3 cash fares at 1:05 p.m. Train Number 25 with engine Number 6 at the head end would leave Redstone at 4:20 p.m. with caboose Number 2 and one car of merchandise off the CB&Q to arrive in Marble at 5:12 p.m. At this time one train operation per day of the Crystal River Railroad would carry the traffic on down to Carbondale to interchange with the D&RG.

During 1911, Roy Coombs fired the Treasury Mountain Shay Railroad's locomotive Number 1 for two or three weeks over the CR&SJ while the 6-spot was being reflued. Extra running time was probably allowed for the run between Marble and Redstone because of the slow speed of this type engine.

Crimes were few in the Crystal River district, but at one time word got around about a planned train robbery. The CR&SJ was carrying a payroll of $100,000.00 at this time with Bill McManus as engineer. He took the precaution to hide the payroll in the sand-box on the engine. Fortunately the robbery didn't materialize. At this time agitators were sent in by rival companies to help stir up the strikes during 1909 and 1910.

In 1917, the Colorado Midland was making extensive plans to run trackage into Carbondale where a station, roundhouse and repair shops were supposed to be built the following spring. The division point at Basalt was short on space and the large amount of land available at Carbondale was thought to be an answer to this problem. However, the U. S. Government took over operations of the Colorado Midland Railroad during World War I and ran operations into the ground

PHOTO BY THE LATE JOHN B. SCHUTTE

Looking down from the original McClures Pass road in 1950, the main east-west range of the Elk Mountains rises boldly into the cool Colorado air above timberline. The Crystal River flows placidly into the settlement of Placita -- just out of sight to the left -- and the CR&SJ railroad grade runs up the valley to the right of the river. Shown here denuded of its ties and rail, the abandoned railway grade has been converted into a State highway (Route 133). The town of Marble is around the hill in the foreground -- tucked into the base of the mountains.

to such an extent that the railroad could not recover to resume operations.

1917-1922 train operations ceased.

On November 18, 1924, the Marble company stock was sold and the Tennessee-Colorado Marble Company resumed operations with former employees. On July 2, 1925, the properties were returned to Colorado Consolidated Yule Marble Company, due in large measure to the fire that destroyed the fabricating mill, April 21, 1925. The loss in machinery and equipment in Shops Number 3 and 4, and Mill "B", together with the buildings, amounted to $531,000. During this period, the Federal Reserve Bank Building of Denver was being constructed with this firm's marble and was completed under most adverse conditions with but a minimum amount of delay.

On December 20, 1927, Jacob Francis Smith got a lease/purchase agreement with the Marble Company, a subsidiary. On December of 1929, the company became solely owned by Vermont Marble Company.

The Placita coal mine was operating in 1930 with an output of 500 cars for the railroad. That year 150 cars of potatoes, 100 cars of stock and 85 cars of marble were delivered to the D&RGW. Incoming carloads of sand for the marble mill and miscellaneous supply items made up the upgrade traffic.

During the depression year of 1931, the 40-pound iron rail was replaced with 75-pound steel. At this time the old wooden railroad bridge at Redstone was replaced with steel, even though the timbers were sound. The coal shipments dropped to 180 carloads this year with 210 cars of livestock, 67 cars of potatoes and 30 cars of marble.

The Placita mine closed in 1932 and only 290 car loads of stock, potatoes and marble rounded off railroad shipments that year. At this time a gasoline-powered motor car with trailer was purchased for $11,000 to handle passengers and mail. The motor car was given the Number A-6. It cost $50.00 per trip to operate one of the steam engines. The gas motor reduced this cost to $10.00 per trip. The section crew was reduced to a foreman and one man on each end of the line. Three round trips were made to Carbondale each week, and the fare was $2.10 one way. The company considered the railroad a necessary evil.

During the fall of 1933, a second trailer was purchased for the Fairmont-engined motor car.

In 1934, a second-hand coach was purchased from the Clarendon & Pittsford and numbered 9. This was purchased to replace the combine probably purchased earlier from the Saratoga & Encampment RR., which was owned by Penn-Wyoming Copper Co. at that time.

The CR&SJ showed a loss on their railroad operations in 1936. At this time a July mudslide covered 600 feet of track to a depth of 6 feet. A "Quick Way" shovel was purchased to do the cleanup work on slides, and this proved to be a worthwhile investment during the last years of operations. The many mudslides during the summer and fall could never be diverted

without great expense. During this year the railroad also purchased two steel air dump cars to ballast the right-of-way. Engine Number 1 was in need of many parts and some extensive rebuilding, so it was decided to purchase the Clarendon & Pittsford's Number 6 locomotive to replace her. The C & P engine was hauled in, pony trucks were added and she was designated Number 3.

In 1926, the engine-house burned to the ground and this required the locomotives to be stored out in the harsh winter weather. To eleviate this problem, the steam plant was cleared out and track was laid into it in 1939 to become the new engine-house.

One of the longest trains on the CR&SJ was a stock movement of 31 cars in 1939. Beavers were a problem along the right of way south of Placita. The beavers would dam up the river so high the track was in danger of being submerged along this low lying area. The railroad called in the state militia to do away with the beavers instead of transplanting them to an area where they could do good. The fall was extremely dry which made it necessary to patrol the track with the pop car after each trip with the steam engine.

In 1940 almost daily runs were made with the steam engines during the fall because of stock movements.

The Vermont Marble Company was forced to install 4,419 ties before the sale because the roadbed was in too poor of a condition to haul out the mill machinery. The railroad was always in a state of extreme deferred maintenance during the

Called out in the winter of 1908, the Crystal River Railroad's rotary snowplow heads for Marble while opening the line through McClures Flats. The CRR probably called on the D&RG for one of the two engines pushing the plow; the CR&SJ's engine would have been marooned at Marble.

last years of operation. This caused constant derailments forcing the company to discourage women and children from riding the railroad. This state of affairs was mainly due to the use of untreated ties, and very little ballast. Traffic was so brisk in the fall that both engines were used in daily shipments of marble and stock. One train consisted of 26 cars of stock. New wheels were installed on the tenders of both engines because the old ones were worn so thin.

Then in 1941 Yule operations were to cease near the end of that year. Morse Brothers Machinery Co. of Denver made the best bid for the CR&SJ personal property and trackage of $15,000. The Interstate Commerce Commission granted permission for abandonment September 22, 1941. Then Morse Brothers took over operations on November 15, 1941.

Morse Brothers Machinery reached Carbondale during January, 1943 with the last train of scrap from the Crystal River Valley.

MARBLE AND THE LINCOLN MEMORIAL

"The Colorado marble is pure white, and therefore it is the most fitting for the Memorial . . . and, even if the cost of the Colorado product should be higher, we favor obtaining it, for it is the handsomest marble we can find." -- William H. Taft, Chairman of the Lincoln Memorial Commission.

The Colorado-Yule Marble Company obtained the Lincoln Memorial contract in 1914. In the extensive Yule Creek Marble beds, 13 separate grades of the stone have been identified by the United States Geological Survey -- ranging from pure white through light green to brown and dark blue-black. Colorado-Yule marble was marketed in five different grades -- although only three grades were considered of superior quality. The three highest grades were -- (1) Statuary "Golden Vein" -- a third grade statuary marble, white with "golden" veining (streaked with colored veins averaging less than one-quarter inch thick and running from yellow to tan in hue). (2) Veined "Colorado Cloud" -- a second grade statuary marble, white with a slight amount of clouding or veining, (3) Pure White Statuary -- top grade white statuary marble with little or no veining, the highest quality marble available. The other two grades of marble sold by Colorado-Yule were variations of the "Golden Vein" type, having irregularities in coloration.

The marble outcroppings along Yule Creek were exposed to view during the great glacial period. For thousands of years this stone has been subject to sudden variations of heat, cold and moisture. Yet throughout all of these severe climatic conditions, the only effect that can be seen there is a slight brownish crust, only slightly thicker than a sheet of paper, where vegetable matter became caked onto the surface of the marble-without having any effect on the stone itself.

The quality of the highest grade white Yule marble has no equal anywhere in the entire world. One critic described it as resembling the purity of new-fallen snow in the wilderness. This is no exaggeration. Yule marble differs in texture and in chemical combination from any other marble yet discovered. In its appearance it resembles the Parian and Carrara marbles, although it is much harder and more durable. These are Old World marbles from which the classic masterpieces of the Greeks and Romans were carved. Father Time has been unable to find a vulnerable point through more than 20-centuries. The texture of Yule marble permits a highly beautiful polish to be applied and its chemical composition is proof against disintegration or discoloration from absorption.

CR&SJ Number 1 appears to be snowbound at first glance in this picture. Photographed after the heavy snowfall during the winter of 1916, Number 1 was actually moving through a "snow cut" at McClure Flats. This was always a likely place for blowing snow to collect, making it necessary to bring out the rotary snow plow to open the line.

Dropping downgrade from Camp Genter, the Crystal River & San Juan's last train is shown being hauled out of Marble during the summer of 1942. This extra consisted of CR&SJ Number 1, Number 2, coach Number 9, two Yule Tram electric motors and two Y.T. flat cars. Engine Number 3 was scrapped on the spot at Marble.

Photographed during the fall of 1966, Lily Lake on the hillside -- east of Camp Genter -- reflects the beauty of Whitehouse Mountain and Treasure Mountain. A White River National Forest guard station is located above its shores, offering protection for the area. All around the lake, wild animals hunt and play in the brush and forest, while beavers keep busy gnawing down aspen trees -- hauling them into the lake to use for food and building materials.

Heading upgrade on May 17, 1925, a CR&SJ mixed train stops momentarily at Camp Genter on its way to Marble. The combination coach-caboose is Number 01 which had been purchased from the Crystal River Railroad -- retaining the original CRR number. This car was 40-feet in length, carried 28 passengers and had a baggage section approximately 8-feet long. It was built in 1901 and was typical of several combination cars built for CF&I-owned railroads.

Camp Genter was located a short distance below the grade to Marble where the track curved off to the east toward Marble. Anthracite coal was mined here for a short time in the 1925 era. The CR&SJ mainline is in the foreground with the mine siding by it. The pit cars at the top carried off the tailings for dumping.

COLLECTION OF THE LATE WILLIAM MCMANUS

COLLECTION OF MAURINE BARNES HERMAN

Farther up the hillside from Lily Lake is another smaller pond that affords a magnificent view of Chair Mountain to the southwest. This pond is rather unusual being at an elevation of nearly 10,000 feet with bull rushes growing from its waters. It is also home for many frogs and other water creatures.

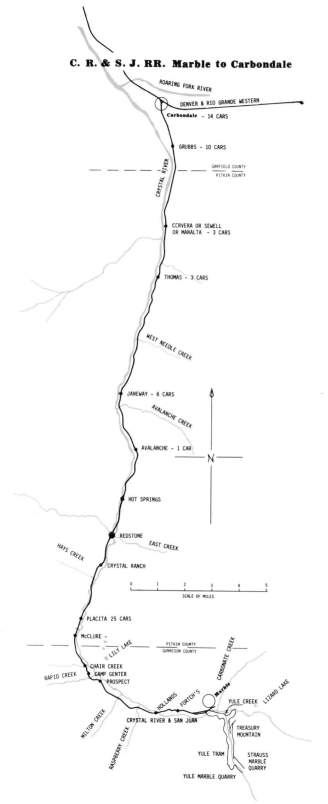

C. R. & S. J. RR. Marble to Carbondale

ROARING FORK RIVER

DENVER & RIO GRANDE WESTERN

Carbondale - 14 CARS

GRUBBS - 10 CARS

GARFIELD COUNTY
PITKIN COUNTY

CRYSTAL RIVER

CERVERA OR SEWELL
OR MANALTA - 3 CARS

THOMAS - 3 CARS

WEST NEEDLE CREEK

JANEWAY - 6 CARS

AVALANCHE CREEK

AVALANCHE - 1 CAR

N

HOT SPRINGS

REDSTONE

EAST CREEK

HAYS CREEK

CRYSTAL RANCH

0 1 2 3 4 5
SCALE OF MILES

PLACITA 25 CARS

McCLURE -

LILY LAKE

PITKIN COUNTY
GUNNISON COUNTY

CHAIR CREEK

CAMP GENTER

RAPID CREEK

PROSPECT

HOLLANDS

FORTCH'S

CARBONATE CREEK

YULE CREEK

LIZARD LAKE

MILTON CREEK

CRYSTAL RIVER & SAN JUAN

TREASURY
MOUNTAIN

RASPBERRY CREEK

YULE TRAM

STRAUSS
MARBLE
QUARRY

YULE MARBLE QUARRY

CR&SJ Number 2 is shown here returning to Marble on September 6, 1941, with empty stock cars. Following the engine is one of the side-dump cars purchased in the late 1930's. The train is about to clatter over the grade crossing at Camp Genter.

CRYSTAL RIVER & SAN JUAN

	train no. 21		STATIONS		train no. 22	
lv.	7:45	a.m.	CARBONDALE	ar.	7:00	p.m.
ar.	8:55	"	REDSTONE	"	5:45	"
"	9:05	"	CRYSTAL RANCH	"	5:39	"
"	9:15	"	PLACITA	"	5:31	"
"	9:20	"	McCLURES	"	5:25	"
"	9:30	"	CHAIR CREEK	"	5:18	"
"	9:35	"	PROSPECT	"	5:14	"
"	9:45	"	HOLLAND	"	5:09	"
"	5:53	"	FORTCH'S	"	5:04	"
"	10:00	"	MARBLE	lv.	5:00	a.m.

1922

The "big snow" of 1916 provided the photographer with a nice Christmas card scene -- featuring CR&SJ Number 1 pulling the combination coach-caboose.

Kline Falls cascades down a narrow gorge near the western edge of Marble in this scene photographed c. 1912. Waterfalls are common along the Crystal River, carrying the melting snows down the precipitous slopes of the Elk Mountains.

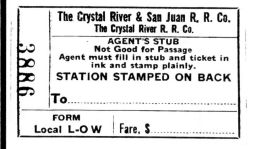

The CR&SJ issued tickets printed on the face side only. This one was found many years ago under the Placita depot. Notice that it is lettered for both the Crystal River & San Juan RR. Co. and the Crystal River RR. Co.

In this autumn color view, an arm of Chair Mountain rises above the valley of the Crystal River at Fortches Ranch. The grade of the CR&SJ is barely visible at the edge of the aspen forest.

PHOTO BY THE LATE JOHN B. SCHUTTE

Chair Creek went on a rampage after a heavy downpour one summer day in 1908. CR&SJ 2-6-0 Number 6 has been forced to a halt with the return to Marble from Redstone. Crystal River RR combine Number 02 was being used at this time. The two railroads were interchanging freight and passengers at Redstone during this period, and ran passenger cars through from Marble to Carbondale. This little engine was affectionately called "The 6-Spot".

Slate Creek was up to its usual tricks in July of 1930. The company spent $600.00 to clear the CR&SJ track of mud and rock with hired, willing backs from the mill and town of Marble.

COLLECTION OF JOHN T. HERMAN

COLLECTION OF THE LATE WILLIAM MCMANUS

As portrayed on a crisp February afternoon, White House Mountain rises in the background above the town of Marble. The "6-Spot" clatters over the Crystal River on a short bridge span heading for Redstone with the second shipment of marble of the day. The bridge pilings were made of marble, which proved it's value as a building material.

"*Winter Marble Shipment*"　　WATERCOLOR PAINTING BY DELL A. MCCOY　123

PHOTO BY MORRISON A. SMITH, COLLECTION OF JOHN W. MAXWELL

CR&SJ Number 1 pulls out of Marble, October 25, 1941, loaded with marble for distant markets. The two steel air dump cars are loaded with crushed marble, followed by two boxcars, loaded with finished marble. Coach Number 9 brings up the rear -- her Baker heater adding to the pall of smoke Number 1 was pouring out to mix with low-lying clouds on this cool and damp autumn day.

The finishing mill of the Colorado Yule Marble Company was in full production when this photograph was taken in the summer of 1912. A marble retaining wall had been placed against the north bank of the Crystal River. This was later built higher to deflect snowslides that roared down the mountain each spring. The railroad cars on the sidings were those of the Chicago & North Western, Grand Trunk, Pacific Fruit Express, Rock Island, Colorado Midland, as well as the Crystal River Railroad's combine coach-caboose Number 02. The CR&SJ's waycar Number 01 can be seen near the far end of the yard.

WESTERN COLLECTION DENVER PUBLIC LIBRARY, PHOTO BY L. C. McCLURE

1992. COLO. YULE MARBLE CO. PLANT N. MARBLE, COLO.
PHOTO BY L.C. McCLURE, DENVER.

The marble finishing mill and railroad were new when this photo was shot at Marble during the spring of 1907. The flags mounted on the smokebox of CR&SJ Number 6 indicates a special trainload of dignitaries had come to visit. The mill was still under construction at this time.

The caption for this photo printed in 1909 reads, "A solid trainload of finished marble leaving local yards". Bridge pilings have been driven into the ground to form the start of the Crystal River bridge later used for the electric tram. The mill is behind the row of reefers and box cars.

CRYSTAL RIVER & SAN JUAN RAILROAD COMPANY						
21	23		STATIONS		22	24
1:35	5:55	lv.	REDSTONE	ar.	5:50	1:30
1:42	6:02	"	CRYSTAL RANCH	"	5:44	1:22
1:54	6:14	"	PLACITA	"	5:34	1:10
1:59	6:19	"	McCLURES	"	5:30	1:06
2:09	6:29	"	CHAIR CREEK	"	5:20	12:53
2:14	6:34	"	PROSPECT	"	5:16	12:48
2:23	6:43	"	HOLLANDS	"	5:10	12:39
2:26	6:46	"	FORTCH'S	"	5:05	12:36
2:30	6:50	ar.	MARBLE	"	5:00	12:30

JULY 1909   RR RED BOOK

The finishing mill and engine terminal at Marble were still under construction when this photograph was taken in 1907. The rail stacked beside the grade was for laying one-mile of track. The attractive emblem on the side of way-car Number 01 was lettered with the initials C. Y. M. for Colorado Yule Marble. The Y. is obscured in the design. The coupler on the way-car was a special interim design permitting the coupling of either link-and-pin or automatic couplers. Notice the added water section on the tender of the 6-Spot that was originally a slope-back tender. The oil head-lamp on the way-car assisted in night switching which was practiced on the CR&SJ at this time.

Looking to the west on December 17, 1909, the turntable at Marble had just been completed. In the background, an electric train can be seen passing the signal tower at the crossing -- on its way to the quarry. This was probably the only turntable pit in the world that was lined with marble.

The Colorado-Yule Marble emblem was reproduced from an embossed advertising sheet printed about 1912.

In the summer of 1915, the station grounds in Marble were a busy place. Special trains came from the East, transporting potential stock buyers. The Colorado Yule Marble Company proudly showed off the shops in the mill and at the end of the day a huge fish fry was held for one and all. Most of these extra trains were brought in by D&RG locomotives.

The late Rome Isler of Marble stands proudly by the A6 ''Pop Car'' he operated as section foreman for the CR&SJ. A water bag was carried for drinking and emergency water for the gasoline engine's radiator. The cast arms nearly touching the rail, knocked fallen rock off the railheads.

PHOTO BY MORRISON A. SMITH, COLLECTION OF JOHN W. MAXWELL

COLLECTION OF MR. AND MRS. CHARLES ORLOSKY

This view shows the "pop car" stopped near the turntable on October 11, 1941. One of the electric tram motors is at the loading platform in the distance.

The depot in Marble was a simple slab-sided building -- with pealing bark. Marble was situated at 7950-feet above sea level, according to the signboard carved in marble. The notice on the door gives train arrivals and departures. The practice was to pay the conductor once on board. This practice made it unnecessary to have a station agent.

In the view at right -- photographed in 1932 -- the Marble depot sits to the left of the tracks. The gas motor-car with trailer was purchased for $11,000 to handle passengers and mail. A round-trip using a steam engine cost $50.00 and a round-trip with the gas motor cost only $10.00. Three round trips were being made to Carbondale each week. The crossing signal tower stands above the other sheds to the right of the depot. A model "A" motor was installed in 1933.

Colo. & Wyo. Form 190. 12-08—200B—108L.

Section Train No. 22
Engine No. 6 — Cooper — Engineer
From Marble — To Redstone
Engine No. — Engineer
From — To
Left Marble at 5:30 A.M.
Arrived at Redstone at 5:45 A.M.

Fireman Coombs
Flagman
Brakeman
Brakeman
Brakeman
Conductor Williams
Date Oct 29 1910
Date Oct 29 1910

KIND OF CARS	LINE INITIAL	ROAD INITIAL	CAR NUMBERS		TAKEN AT No.	LEFT AT No.	DESTINATION No.	KIND OF LOAD	GROSS TONS	CONDITIONS OF SEALS AND CAR FASTENINGS			
			EMPTY	LOADED						A. Door	B. Door	C. Door	D. Door

Colo. & Wyo. Form 190. 12-08—200B—100L.

Section Train No. 22 + 2
Engine No. 701 — Cooper — Engineer
From — To
Engine No. — Engineer
From — To
Left — at 8:20 A.M.
Arrived at — at M.

Fireman Coombs
Flagman
Brakeman
Brakeman
Brakeman
Conductor Williams
Date 1/1 1911
Date 1/1 1911

KIND OF CARS	LINE INITIAL	ROAD INITIAL	CAR NUMBERS		TAKEN AT No.	LEFT AT No.	DESTINATION No.	KIND OF LOAD	GROSS TONS	CONDITIONS OF SEALS AND CAR FASTENINGS			
			EMPTY	LOADED						A. Door	B. Door	C. Door	D. Door

These prints were copied from a conductor's book that holds treasured memories of early railroad movements on the CR&SJ. Dated October 29, 1910, William McManus was conductor and brakeman along with Cooper as engineer and Roy Coombs as fireman. Marble to Redstone and return twice a day was the order of business. By January 1, 1911, the motive power was the leased C&W 701 with the same crew and Ross added as brakeman for the longer run into Carbondale and back. Snow-fighting equipment was the order of the day.

130

COLLECTION OF THE REV. MORRIS CAFKY

Crystal River & San Juan Railroad

TRI-WEEKLY DIVISION

TRAIN SHEET

TUESDAY THURSDAY SATURDAY

Time Table No. ___   Marble, Colo., APRIL 16   1940

EASTBOUND			Distance	TRAIN	Distance	2 / 1	WESTBOUND	
				TRAIN		2 1		
				ENGINE		1		
				CONDUCTOR SMITH				
				BRAKEMAN SMITH				
				ENGINEER CHIDESTER				
				FIREMAN WALTHER				
				TIME ORDERED FOR 8:00A				
Dep	**Dep**	**Dep** 7:15 A	0	MARBLE TOW	27.5	**Ar** 2:00 P	**Ar**	**Ar**
			7.4					
		7:46 A	7.4	PLACITA	20.1	1:35 P		
			3.5					
		8:10 A	10.9	REDSTONE YW	16.6	12:50 P		
			6.1					
		8:35 A	17	JANEWAY	10.5	12:15 P		
			5.9					
		8:55 A	22.9	SEWELL	4.6	11:50 A		
			2.9					
		9:05 A	25.8	GRUBBS	1.7	11:40 A		
			1.7					
Ar	**Ar**	**Ar** 9:15 A	27.5	CARBONDALE Y	0	**Dep** 11:30 A	**Dep**	**Dep**

COLLECTION OF ROBERT RICHARDSON

COLLECTION OF ESTHER SANCHEZ

This train schedule was usually tacked on a door near the depot site during the last years of operation.

Esther and two other Marble teenagers wave farewell to the end of an era from the platform of combination baggage-coach Number 9, in 1942.

The Marble depot signboard was mounted for many years on the pop stand run by Theresa Francis. It had been hand carved by the skilled hands of some unknown marble craftsman.

DELL A. MCCOY

Marble was a boom town when this photo was taken in 1911. The CR&SJ had recently purchased the Crystal River Railroad's rotary snowplow and combine coach-caboose -- spotted behind the engine house along with CR&SJ engine Number 6. The Treasury Mountain Railroad grade was almost new and is seen to the right. The electric tram line is to the left and the smoke is coming from the power-house chimney. This view looks down river to the west. This engine house was formerly the barn used by teamsters that hauled marble down by wagon using four to six horse teams.

Throughout the abandonment of the marble works and railroad during the winter of 1942, numerous trainloads of scrap went out of Marble. A wedge plow had been bolted onto the pilot beam of Number 1 to keep the drifts cleared out. One of the Yule Tram electric motors sits at the loading platform in the background.

This panoramic view shows the finishing mill of the Colorado Yule Marble Company at Marble in the summer of 1914. This photo was taken shortly after completion of this structure which measured one-fourth of a mile in length. Company owned houses are above the mill, and the Crystal River flows past in the foreground. Shop Number 3 is to the far left. Next in line was Mill B with 22 gang saws. Following that were the diamond saws and rubbing beds in Shop Number 2. Eight more gang saws followed this in Mill A. In the Number 1 machine shop, a display room was alongside the white painted office.

The tall building to the rear of the mill was constructed as Shop Number 4 to house the fluting machines used to produce the columns of the Lincoln Memorial. An extra siding had been run along the back of the craneway for dumping waste marble to be used in strengthening the supports of the traveling crane. This was necessary because of the tremendous tonnage involved in the Lincoln Memorial stonework.

The small white building in the foreground contained the excelsior mill. This was wood shavings used for packing marble. A storehouse and a blacksmith shop were alongside the track as well as a small scale shed equipped with a weighing track.

Several box cars are being loaded on the house track alongside the mill. The main line is the center track and Number 01 combine coach-caboose is on the passing track. Another spur runs along the backside of the marble wall, next to the river. This had been constructed recently to ward off snowslides that roared down off Mt. Wood.

As shown above, Carbonate Creek flows from timberline down through the bare cut and on past the business district to the right. Carbonate Creek has dangerous mud slides that occur nearly every year, caused by heavy rains. It was one of these mud slides that finally wiped out many houses and main street buildings in its path in 1941.

The white shed alongside the electric line -- in the center of the picture -- was the oil house. The electric loading platform is to the right of this. A pine tree hides the Marble depot next to the signal tower at the crossing. To the right of this crossing stands the electric shop. Just visible over the engine is the turntable pit, with the engine-house hidden behind the power plant. The Crystal River bridge carried the electric tram to the quarry.

The pride of the CR&SJ rests in the engine house at Marble, September 6, 1941, waiting for her next run. It was nearly the last year of operation before Number 1 had a roof over her head due to the fire that burned the original engine house to the ground in 1926.

The Marble terminal was quiet on this winter day in 1940. Passenger car Number 9 sits on the Treasury Mountain RR. lead track -- and near the center, one of the electric tram motors rests on the siding, while farther to the right, engine Number 1 is spotted beside the shovel (called the "go devil"). The enginehouse is in back of the electric motor. In this view the photographer was looking toward the east.

In 1926, the original enginehouse (a former barn) burned to the ground -- with CR&SJ Number 1 inside. The railroad did without an engine house after this fire until 1940 when the steam plant was made over for that purpose. During this period, it was necessary to do repairs out doors. Notice the ventilator stack that slipped over the smokestack.

The CR&SJ enginehouse had finally been completed in 1940, using what had been the steam power-house. This resulted in a large saving in coal and repairs. Due to the long winters, it was difficult to make repairs out-of-doors. CR&SJ Number 1 and Number 2 rest in their new stalls in this picture.

Photographed in 1937 by his father, Del Gerbaz leans out of the cab of CR&SJ Number 3 at Marble. This engine came from the Claredon & Pittsford as Number 6. Although this engine arrived to replace the worn CR&SJ Number 1, records do not indicate that Number 3 operated for more than one year. Notice the Fox trucks under the tender.

CR&SJ Number 3 rusts away in the peaceful mountain surroundings east of the mill -- in September of 1941. Number 3 had been cast aside on the old Treasury Mountain Railroad interchange track -- minus headlight, bell and other vital parts. In the next year, Morse Brothers Machinery cut her up on the spot for salvage. In the late 1960's the remains of her firebox and crown sheet still marked the spot where she died.

138

During the rehabilitating of the Marble finishing mill in 1922, the large steel building shown in this view had been built. This duochrome also shows the immense size of the snow slide wall built to protect the mill. The overall mill operation is in a sad state of repair at this time -- in 1934, in the midst of the Great Depression. CR&SJ Number 2 is on the house track, along with a second-hand combine purchased from the Saratoga & Encampment. Combine coach Number 9 sits near the unpainted office.

The Treasury Mountain Railroad track came into Marble on the track on the left side of this photograph. The former CR&SJ enginehouse sat next to this grade and the enginehouse, as of the date of the photo, was to the right. The gas motor-car was housed in the center shed, and the turntable is behind this.

Shown at the right are two maps of the railroad terminal and mill grounds at Marble. The 1915 era was a period when marble was a supreme choice in the building field by architects. The 1940 map illustrates the mill as a shadow of it's former greatness and the engine terminal had changed with the effects of time.

Marble Terminal Before 1915

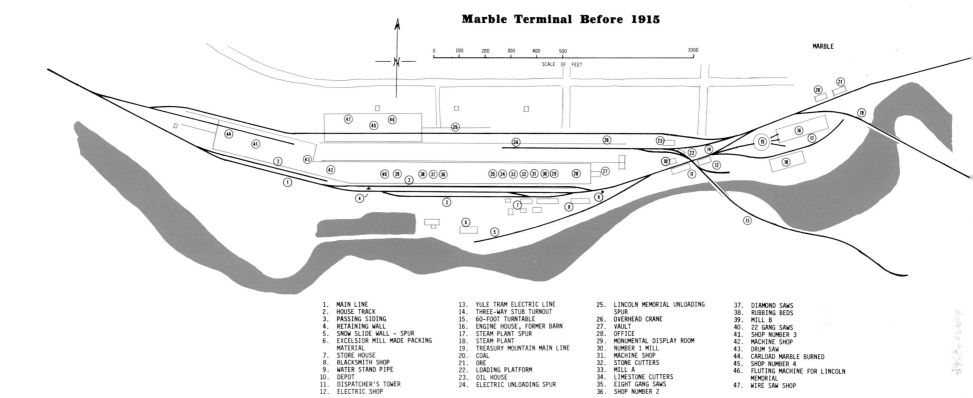

1. MAIN LINE	13. YULE TRAM ELECTRIC LINE	25. LINCOLN MEMORIAL UNLOADING	37. DIAMOND SAWS
2. HOUSE TRACK	14. THREE-WAY STUB TURNOUT	SPUR	38. RUBBING BEDS
3. PASSING SIDING	15. 60-FOOT TURNTABLE	26. OVERHEAD CRANE	39. MILL B
4. RETAINING WALL	16. ENGINE HOUSE, FORMER BARN	27. VAULT	40. 22 GANG SAWS
5. SNOW SLIDE WALL - SPUR	17. STEAM PLANT SPUR	28. OFFICE	41. SHOP NUMBER 3
6. EXCELSIOR MILL MADE PACKING	18. STEAM PLANT	29. MONUMENTAL DISPLAY ROOM	42. MACHINE SHOP
MATERIAL	19. TREASURY MOUNTAIN MAIN LINE	30. NUMBER 1 MILL	43. DRUM SAW
7. STORE HOUSE	20. COAL	31. MACHINE SHOP	44. CARLOAD MARBLE BURNED
8. BLACKSMITH SHOP	21. ORE	32. STONE CUTTERS	45. SHOP NUMBER 4
9. WATER STAND PIPE	22. LOADING PLATFORM	33. MILL A	46. FLUTING MACHINE FOR LINCOLN
10. DEPOT	23. OIL HOUSE	34. LIMESTONE CUTTERS	MEMORIAL
11. DISPATCHER'S TOWER	24. ELECTRIC UNLOADING SPUR	35. EIGHT GANG SAWS	47. WIRE SAW SHOP
12. ELECTRIC SHOP		36. SHOP NUMBER 2	

Marble Terminal 1940

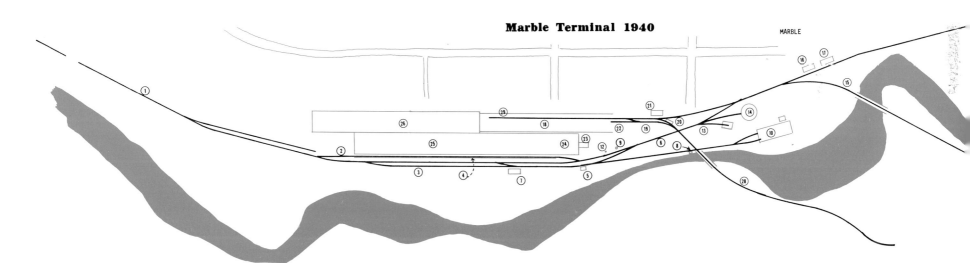

1. MAIN LINE	11. WATER STAND PIPE	21. OIL HOUSE
2. HOUSE TRACK	12. THREE-WAY STUB TURNOUT	22. ELECTRIC ROTARY SPUR
3. PASSING SIDING	13. "POP" CAR SHED	23. VAULT
4. RETAINING WALL	14. 60-FOOT TURNTABLE	24. MILL OFFICE
5. SCALE HOUSE	15. TREASURY MOUNTAIN TRACK	25. MILL SHOPS
6. ENGINE HOUSE LEAD	16. SAND	26. LOADING SHED
7. STORE HOUSE	17. COAL	27. MILL SHOPS
8. OUT HOUSE	18. ELECTRIC UNLOADING SPUR	28. YULE TRAM ELECTRIC LINE
9. GAS PUMP FOR "POP" CAR	19. PASSING SIDING	29. OVERHEAD CRANE
10. ENGINE HOUSE	20. LOADING PLATFORM	

"The Marble Booster" hummed with activity in 1915. Job printing and a weekly newspaper kept the staff busy. The upper view shows a pressman running one of the hand-fed platen presses, while the editor Frank Frost and his wife, sit at the wrapping table writing copy. Typesetting often ended up as over-time work so the pressman could do his job the next shift. The typesetting department was operated by the same staff pictured in the view to the right.

THE CRYSTAL RIVER AND SAN JUAN RAILROAD COMPANY

1932   **29**

PASS   Mr. C. D. Pierce,
Account C. F. A.,
C. B. & Q. R. R. Co.

UNTIL DECEMBER 31, 1932, UNLESS OTHERWISE ORDERED OR SPECIFIED
HEREON, AND SUBJECT TO CONDITIONS ON BACK.
VALID WHEN COUNTERSIGNED BY WALTER W. BLOOD OR W. F. HAFNER;

COUNTERSIGNED

W.F. Hafner

Maurice W Blood

SECRETARY

CONDITIONS:

This is a free pass. based upon no consideration whatever, and it may be revoked at any time, and if presented by any person other than the individual named hereon, or if any alteration, addition or erasure is made upon it, it is forfeited and the conductor will take it up and collect full fare. The person accepting and using this pass, in consideration of receiving the same, assumes all risk of accident and expressly agrees that The Crystal River and San Juan Railroad Company shall not be held liable to any person whomsoever under any circumstances, whether of negligence, criminal or otherwise, of its agents or others, for any injury to the person or for any loss or damage to the property of the individual using this pass. and that as to such person the railroad shall not be considered a common carrier or liable as such.

I hereby assent to the above statement, and agree that this pass is subject to the above conditions.

I hereby represent that I am not prohibited by law from receiving this pass, and agree that it will be lawfully used.

This pass will not be honored unless signed in ink by the person to whom issued.

The partners, Hoffman & Tischauseer built this small smelter at the edge of Marble (on the south side of the Crystal River) in 1898. The operation lasted only a short time due primarily to the relatively poor grades of ore encountered in the district. The partner's lack of knowledge in metallurgy also contributed to the failure of this enterprise. Gold, silver, lead and zinc ores were processed here.

The passes issued during the Great Depression expressed the simplicity of that era in their printing. They were printed in a plain and straightforward way -- unlike the gaudy passes of the "Gay Nineties" and "Roaring Twenties".

Sub-zero winter air, steam and snow combine to make a chilly atmospheric shot of CR&SJ Number 1 at Marble in 1927, after rebuilding -- following the engine house fire. This was when she acquired a wedge-plow -- mounted on the pilot beam -- for plowing out light snow drifts.

Fresh-fallen snow in the Rockies can make a beautiful, but awesome and unforgettable scene. In this blue duochrome, White House mountain rises in the background, and the Crystal River bridge of the electric tram is to the left. CR&SJ Number 1 sends up clouds of steam in the crisp frigid air of Marble in this midwinter photo taken in 1932.

This view shows one of the traveling cranes -- loaded in a steel mill-gondola -- being shipped out of Marble for use in the South. The Texaco gas pump was used to fuel the pop-car. This load was moved in March of 1942.

This open-end observation car was one of eleven private cars that were pulled into Marble in 1912. The coach had been backed onto the Treasury Mountain track.

The mill yard at Marble was nearly filled with blocks of marble on October 11, 1941. The traveling crane operators didn't like to work their loads around the piles of marble when the yard became so full. The craneway was 70-feet wide and 1,260-feet long.

The Marble Mill had closed in 1917 -- and the CR&SJ had not run a train for nearly five years. Then in 1922, the mill was reopened, and on July 24, 1924, the previous owners, the Yule Marble Company and the Carrara Company, agreed to merge into the Consolidated Yule Marble Company -- which then joined with the Tennessee-Colorado Marble Company. The new company was going great until a fire broke out in Shop No. 3 on April 21, 1925. The fire gained tremendous headway and the townspeople could do little to fight the fire because the water supply system was under repair. Over 900-feet of the mill was a complete loss, along with this flat-car load of finished grave markers worth $10,000.00. This car was being loaded inside Shop No. 3. The fire probably was deliberately started by outside interests.

PHOTO BY MORRISON A. SMITH, COLLECTION OF JOHN W. MAXWELL

146

COLLECTION OF MR. AND MRS. CHARLES ORLOSKY

Colonel Meek was born at Mt. Pleasant, Iowa, on September 26, 1855. At the age of thirteen he left his home and supported himself from that time. While working for the Rock Island Railroad, he learned telegraphy and through this he became interested in railroading. After a trip through California he accepted a position with the Rock Island as chief dispatcher, and in 1882 he was appointed general superintendent of the St. Louis, Des Moines & Northern Railroad and two subsidiary lines. In this position he acquired a wide reputation for ability. In 1887, when the Denver, Texas & Fort Worth Railroad was near completion (now part of Burlington Northern's subsidiary, the Colorado & Southern Railway), he was offered the position of general manager which he accepted. His first official act as manager of this line was to cut all the rates, passenger and freight, 30-percent. This started a rate war with the officers of the transcontinental lines running into Colorado which lasted for several years. During this fight he was successful at every turn, and eventually formed an alliance with the Union Pacific.

Shortly thereafter, the name of the Texas road was changed to the Union Pacific, Denver & Gulf, which name it retained while under U.P. control. Col. Meek continued to work for this railroad until 1891, when he became interested in private ventures in Mexico. At that time he gave up his railraod work to go "south of the border". He was engaged in Mexico

COL. CHANNING F. MEEK

Col. Channing Meek is shown here in 1912 at his desk inside the office at the mill. The office was simple in comparison to other large business offices of the period. By today's standards, the mills operations would require office space several times greater than the spartan facilities found at the marble mill prior to World War I.

for several months and reportedly made a large sum of money while there. He returned to Colorado and for some time interested himself with various companies. Part of this time he was employed by the Colorado Fuel & Iron Company. During the administration of President Harrison he had been offered the general superintendency of the United States railway mail service, but refused. After returning to

Colorado, he became seriously interested in forming a company to produce and market marble building materials. He became aware of the marble deposits on Yule Creek between 1890 and 1893, when serving as president of the Colorado Coal & Iron Company (which later consolidated with J. C. Osgood's Colorado Fuel Company to form the Colorado Fuel & Iron Company). In February of 1905, the Colorado-Yule Marble Company was incorporated in the state of New York by Joseph P. Slensky, Spencer Melton and Maurice Kastriner. During April of the same year Col. Meek approached the company's officers, offering to sell valuable land he owned in the Marble area to the company, in return for the presidency of the firm. The Colorado-Yule Marble Company accepted his offer and he became that company's first truly dynamic president. He served in that capacity until his death in 1912.

MARBLE VIGNETTES

During the spring of 1912 -- on March 20th -- a snowslide came roaring down Mount Wood, smashing into the mill at Marble with tremendous force. Because the slide hit the mill during the change of shifts between the day and night crews, no one was killed. Only the telephone operator was in the building at the time. Over 300 workers could have been in the building at their jobs when the slide hit. The concussion turned over CR&SJ engine Number 6 after the mill had been flattened like a deck of cards. A nearby resident was at his kitchen window when the snow

COL. CHANNING F. MEEK

broke out the window frame and neatly laid it around his head and shoulders!

One of the more colorful characters of Marble was Sylvia Smith, editor of "The Marble City Times". Her newspaper editorials always showed the worst side of the Marble Company -- greatly annoying the business men of Marble, and the management of the Marble Company. She was of the opinion that the Colorado-Yule Marble Company's executive officers were more interested in selling stock to Eastern dudes than they were in establishing markets and selling building stone. When she wrote up the big snowslide in a derogatory fashion -- claiming that the avalanche could have killed hundreds of workers because of the poor placement of the finishing mill -- management of the Marble Company and other business leaders in the town became especially distraught. They called a town meeting where the feelings of nearly 300 residents were inflamed to a point of near-violence. In the end, a resolution was signed by 180 of those present. On the following day a committee presented it to Miss Smith, demanding that she leave Marble and never return. She refused to do so -- as might have been expected -- leading to the illegal actions on the part of the town officials, and ultimately resulting in a court battle. On March 27, 1912, the town marshal was ordered to place Miss Smith aboard the northbound CR&SJ train for Carbondale -- town officials using the pretext that it was unsafe for her to remain in Marble. When she refused to board the train, she was forcibly put aboard and accompanied by the marshal.

Miss Smith did not tarry at Carbondale, however. She boarded a D&RG train for Glenwood Springs with connections to Denver. In Denver, she quickly consulted a lawyer who filed a lawsuit against the Colorado-Yule Marble Company, the Crystal River & San Juan Railroad, the Town of Marble and several of the town's residents.

In April of the following year, Miss Smith was awarded $10,345.00 in damages by the Gunnison County District Court -- which was later sustained by the State Supreme Court. The affair eventually lead many of Marble's residents to harbor grudges against the Marble Company's executives. Colonel Meek had personally assured all of those who took part in the affair that they would not be harmed. However, between the time the suit was filed and the final judgement was rendered, Colonel Meek was killed, and the new Corporate executives refused to honor his pledge. As a result, several Marble residents lost their businesses, others lost their homes and yet others had their wages or bank accounts garnisheed.

COLLECTION OF THE LATE WILLIAM MCMANUS

The Larkin Hotel was clean and comfortable, but by no means stylish. Meals served were A Number One, well cooked and wholesome. The transient rates were $2.50 a day. This hotel was just up the hill from the mill.

The gang truck is loaded with cut-down blocks of marble in this 1909 view shot at the back of the mill. The gang trucks in the rear are ready to be run into the mill under the gang saws.

In this scene photographed in 1910, the mill's 25-ton crane is lifting a block of marble -- 16-ft. x 8-ft. x 2-ft. in size -- to load onto a gang truck. The smaller 15-ton crane is in the distance. Mill doors open to the gang saws.

In the 1909 photo to the right, a column block is readied for the lathe. The block is resting between the rails of the transfer-table track along the back of the mill; it was necessary to chip the squared corners for this operation by hand.

COLLECTION OF THE FRANK GERTIG FAMILY

COLLECTION OF THE LATE WILLIAM MCMANUS

COLLECTION OF THE LATE WILLIAM MCMANUS

The view above, to the left, looks west in Shop Number 3. This photo provides some idea of the size of the working force employed in 1912 to shape the marble. A great deal of hand labor was required at this time, and the workmen were the most skilled in the trade. The Colorado-Yule Marble Company paid the highest wages of any firm in the business.

The Colorado-Yule Marble Company office was a simple building on the hill on Main Street. The sign designated this was the Western Union Telegraph and Cable Co. office, as well.

This workman was busy at the rotary rubbing-bed -- of which the company had 10 in use. The flat surface is a steel disk that revolved and smoothed the surface of marble placed on top of it. The workman was placing 10-pound iron weights on a small block of marble. The rubbing beds were in Shop Number 2.

This was one of the 30 steel frame gang saws at the mill. Each wedge, or "dog", holds one saw of the gang. The saws were straight flat pieces of steel, one-sixteenth-inch by four-inches deep and nine to 16-feet long. The frame carried the saws back and forth, barely touching the marble. The blades lowered automatically on large screws on each side of the frame. Sand, or crushed steel, and water fed from above, caught in the hopper under the gang track and was automatically pumped to the top for use again. The gang trucks came in and out from the yard for easy loading and unloading. A block could be placed under the saws in less than three minutes.

153

Headed for Arlington National Cemetery in Washington, D.C. in February of 1931, this huge block of marble was destined to become the revered Tomb of the Unknown Soldier. This block of marble weighed 56-tons and measured 14-feet, 6-inches by 7-feet, 6-inches by 6-feet, 6-inches. It was the largest block ever quarried in the world. CR&SJ Number 2 pauses momentarily in this publicity photo taken at Marble, Colorado. The block was shipped to Vermont for finishing, received there February 17, 1931.

THE TOMB OF THE UNKNOWN SOLDIER

ARLINGTON NATIONAL CEMETERY, VA.

Erected to honor the memory of all the Nation's unknown war dead.

An unidentified soldier who died in World War I was chosen and enshrined as a representative of the thousands of unknown citizen-soldiers who died in the defense of their country -- and to preserve Freedom, Justice and Equality in the world for all men, regardless of race, creed or color.

155

This was a diamond saw used in cutting blocks to smaller sizes. Four cuts could be made through marble in one minute. A machine like this cost $5,000 to $6,000 when purchased new in 1914.

In Shop Number 1, stone cutters used pneumatic tools to do the fine sculpture work. This was the shop nearest the office.

157

THE LINCOLN MEMORIAL

THE LINCOLN MEMORIAL

". . . that this nation under God shall have a new birth of freedom -- and that government of the people, by the people, for the people shall not perish from the Earth."

From the closing statement of
Abraham Lincoln's Gettysburg Address

If President Abraham Lincoln had been an ordinary political leader -- or even an ordinary national hero -- an ordinary monument would have been sufficient to honor his memory and no doubt a suitable structure would have been promptly erected. However, Lincoln was not ordinary -- far from it -- and more than half a century elapsed before a proper memorial was dedicated to this heroic man of the people whose name has penetrated to the ends of the earth, and is called to mind wherever aspiration kindles the heart or tyranny oppresses mankind. The Lincoln Memorial -- neither palace nor temple nor tomb -- has a unique nature, gathering within its beautiful marble walls the very essence of his upright character, steeped in tolerance and the belief that all people should be free -- free to think, free to express themselves, and free to apply themselves to the enterprises that best allow them to use their God-given talents and abilities to serve their fellow man.

The Lincoln Memorial Commission -- after many delays in the U.S. Congress -- came about in February of 1911, ". . . to secure plans and designs for a Monument or Memorial to the memory of Abraham Lincoln." The Lincoln Memorial came about as a result of the efforts of this Commission.

During the tenth meeting of the Commission, on February 3, 1912, it was decided to locate the Lincoln Memorial in Potomac Park on the axis of the U.S. Capitol and the Washington Monument. Henry Bacon, a New York architect, was chosen to prepare the final design, which Congress approved January 29, 1913. Groundbreaking for the Memorial took place on February 12, 1914, and the cornerstone was laid February 12, 1915. Subsequently, Daniel C. French was selected as sculptor for the statue of Lincoln, and Jules Guerin was chosen to design and execute the murals for the end walls and the ornamentation on the bronze ceiling beams.

On Memorial Day, May 30, 1922, the Lincoln Memorial was officially dedicated and opened to the public.

COLLECTION OF FRED AND JO MAZZULLA

Abraham Lincoln – The Man of the People

"Inasmuch as most things are produced by labor, it follows that all such things rightly belong to those whose labor has produced them.

"But as so often happened in all ages of the world, some have labored and others have without labor, enjoyed a large proportion of the fruits. This is wrong and should not continue.

"To secure to each laborer the whole product of his labor, or as nearly as possible, is a worthy object of any good government."

Abraham Lincoln

159

On the wall above the statue is the following inscription:

"In this temple as in the hearts of the people for whom he saved the Union the memory of Abraham Lincoln is enshrined forever."

The columns for the Lincoln Memorial were finished in Shop Number 4. Looking west inside the shop, one can see a small traveling crane, the CR&SJ's indoor loading track, and several blocks nearing completion. Windows afforded most of the light for the workers.

The Lincoln Memorial was by far the proudest achievement of the Colorado-Yule Marble Company and the citizens of Marble, Colorado. An often overlooked fact concerning this famous Memorial is that Colorado-Yule marble could not have been used for this structure if railroads had not existed to move such great tonnages two-thirds of the way across the United States to Washington, D.C.

The U.S. Commission of Fine Arts, with Daniel C. French as chairman, unanimously voted -- after carefully investigating all the different kinds of marble and other building stone produced in the United States -- that Colorado-Yule marble was "pre-eminently fitted" for the construction of the Lincoln Memorial. This structure was calculated to be one of the most beautiful -- and one of the largest -- monuments ever built, a high tribute to the quality of Colorado-Yule marble.

When the Lincoln Memorial Commission accepted the findings of the Commission of Fine Arts, the chairman of the Memorial Commission, William Howard Taft, noted that, "the Colorado marble is pure white, and therefore it is the most fitting for the Memorial . . . and, even if the cost of the Colorado product should be higher, we favor obtaining it, for it is the handsomest marble we can find."

The exterior of the Lincoln Memorial symbolizes the Grand Union of the United States of America. Around the walls of the Memorial Hall is a colonnade of the States of the Union, the frieze above it bearing the names of the 36 states existing at the time of Lincoln's death. On the attic walls above the colonnade are the names of the 48 states making up the Union at the time the Memorial was built. These walls and great columns enclose the sanctuary containing three memorials to Abraham Lincoln.

The place of honor inside the Memorial is occupied by a colossal marble statue of the Man of the People, himself. This statue of Lincoln was designed and modeled by Daniel C. French, and is in the Central Hall of the Memorial. It represents Lincoln as the Civil War President seated in a great armchair standing 12-1/2 feet high, over the back of which a flag has been draped. Overall, the statue measures 19-feet from head to foot.

The carving of the statue was done by the Piccirrilli Brothers in their New York studio-workshop, where it was also worked on by Daniel French personally. Over six years were devoted to the creation of this work of art.

COLLECTION OF MRS. MAURINE BARNES HERMAN

Some of the finest examples of polished marble were put on display at one of the monument conventions held in Denver many years ago. The desk is made entirely of marble, which must have weighed nearly 500-pounds.

This copy print is of the Municipal Building in New York City. Some 350,000-square-feet of Colorado-Yule Marble was used in the construction of this building.

COLLECTION OF THE LATE WILLIAM MCMANUS

Marble residents were proud of their St. Paul's Episcopal Church. In 1910, a bell tower was added. This building was brought in from Aspen in 1909 on a flat car. The church and reading-room were used by three denominations. A large Aeolian organ worked either manually or mechanically, utilizing perforated music rolls.

The company houses built along the main road into Marble were small, but comfortable. These houses rented for $4.00 per month back in the "good old days". A water hydrant provided outdoor water, while outdoor plumbing was standard.

The larger company houses in Marble rented for $12 to $15 per month. Several of these are still in use today.

A group of Marble teachers posed outside of the Woods' family home on Main Street in 1910. This house was built of split log and could last for many years if the roof was properly cared for.

The Woods' home was hard hit on that black day, August 8, 1941, when a cloudburst turned Carbonate Creek into a wall of mud, rock and water. The hospital buildings and Masonic Temple were badly damaged, along with several homes in the path of the flood. Debris piled up as high as 20-feet in places near the Main Street. The damage would have been staggering if the town were still in the boom years.

Col. Channing Meek had the largest house in Marble shown in this 1911 photograph. Built on a hillside, one could obtain a splendid view from this property -- surveying the mill and town as well as the peaks surrounding the valley. This view looks to the southwest.

In 1913, a spring performance was held by the Marble band beside the bell tower. Note the band uniforms. The large building was the Masonic Temple. An ice cream parlor and Princess Theater was to the right. The air was chilly and snow laid fresh on the peaks -- but this did not end the gay festivities of the day. The electric tram grade may be seen in the background.

At a later time, this group of band performers posed for a group picture with their instruments. A musical performance given in Marble's beautiful setting would linger indefinitely in the minds of the people who attended it.

This photo was taken in 1910 and looks down Main Street in Marble. A small bridge crosses Carbonate Creek, one block down from Main Street -- the pathway of so many mud and rock slides.

A millinery shop was housed in the building to the left. The Post Office is to the far right.

165

COLLECTION OF MRS. MAURINE BARNES HERMAN

COLLECTION OF MR. AND MRS. CHARLES ORLOSKY

In 1925 the Main Street of Marble had many interesting buildings when the Elks Convention came to town.

During 1922, Pat Hanlon was the sheriff of Gunnison County, and this photo shows him sitting in the buggy (on the right). The building in the background was on Marble's Main Street and had a bakery and dry goods "emporium" in it. This may have been one of the sheriff's regular trips to Marble.

The Henry Merton Store at Marble was divided into a jewelry department (to the right), a prescription department (to the rear), and a ladies' toiletries department (to the left). This was about 1914.

Mervin Aude demonstrates one of the best modes of winter transportation in the town of Marble in 1915. At nearly 8,000-feet in elevation, the winters at Marble promised -- and usually delivered -- a lot of snow.

Marble's Main Street looked like a town out of the Old West in this photo taken in 1910. In this view, the photograph looked to the south. The population was approaching 700 and growing rapidly. These buildings later burned in the fire of 1916.

COLLECTION OF MRS. MAURINE BARNES HERMAN

COLLECTION OF MERVIN C. AUDE

COLLECTION OF THE LATE WILLIAM MCMANUS

Sunshine breaks through momentarily on an aspen grove across from Beaver Lake
at the edge of Marble.   Both the Treasury Mountain Railroad and the Yule Tram
followed Yule Creek up into the distant hills to their quarries.

Probably built in 1908, Yule Tram electric motor Number 100 had just arrived in Marble from the quarry. She is in front of the Colorado Yule Marble Company's loading dock in this 1910 view. The marble shed housed oil drums. The track in the foreground was used as a passing siding.

I n 1907, blocks of marble were wagoned down from the quarry to the mill by teamsters who could stop their wagons on a dime with their skillful use of the reins, or "ribbons" as they were called. All this was accomplished on slippery, winding, tipsy roads -- with a heavy foot on the brake. The large barn in Marble served both iron ponies and the teams for the quarry at this time. Then in 1908 a Chase Steam Tractor was brought in to replace the teamsters. The tractor could handle 5 to 7 wagons carrying 12 to 16 tons per wagon. This tractor was built by the Best Manufacturing Company.

On September 21, 1908, the marble company began widening the roadway to 10 feet for the construction of an electric tramway line. This tram line was completed in 1910.

One of the saddest accidents that happened in the Marble area took place on this electric railway. On a train going downgrade from the quarry on Saturday, August 10, 1912, there were seven passengers, including Col. Channing Meek. New brakes had been installed on the trolley and it was customary to apply the brakes

SECTION V CONTINUED ON PAGE 171

This 1908 view shows the marble company's steam tractor with passengers coming across the Crystal River. The roadbed it traveled was used almost exclusively by the electric tram two years later.

Built by the Best Manufacturing Company, this steam tractor replaced horse-drawn wagons for bringing out marble from the Colorado Yule Marble Company's quarry in 1908. Cal Adams was the tractor driver, and he must have been a fearless soul to have had three wagon loads of marble -- weighing 16-tons per wagon -- following him on the extremely steep grades. The steam tractor was used about two seasons before being replaced by the electric tramway.

the entire distance down. For some unexplained reason, while descending the steeper grades, the brakes failed and the train shot down the slope at a terrific speed. Two quarrymen jumped as the train gathered speed, then Col. Meek instructed the others to jump from the train on the inside of a curve just before reaching Marble, where there was a space of about fifteen-feet of level ground. Col. Meek and Mr. Frazier, the general manager of the company, jumped first. Then, as they rounded the curve, the motorman jumped, landing in a hole at the side of one of the electric poles, striking his head. When Col. Meek jumped he landed on his feet, but was thrown forward with great force and was unable to rise. He was in great pain but remained conscious. The others escaped with only minor injuries. In the meantime, the brakes on the train had automatically regained operation and

it came to a halt before the remaining passengers had jumped. Another trolley was sent out to gather up the injured, and once back in Marble, Col. Meek was taken to his home in his automobile. For the next two days he was in great pain, so a doctor was sent for from Denver. Consequently, Dr. Schultz, a specialist from Denver, consulted with Dr. Schmidt of Glenwood Springs and Dr. Swift of Marble, and they concluded that the Colonel's condition was very serious but that very little could be done for him. That Wednesday he began to fail and realizing that he might die, Col. Meek called Mr. Frazier to his side and gave full instruction concerning the carrying on of the work. Shortly after twelve on August 14, 1912, his heart stopped.

This was a terrible shock to the entire population of Marble -- and, in fact, to the entire state of Colorado, for through-

out the state, Colonel Meek was a man recognized as an empire builder, a first citizen and a "man among men".

"The Marble Booster," the local newspaper, in reporting Colonel Meek's death printed the following account on August 17, 1912: "The Colorado-Yule Marble Company was the child of Colonel Meek's dreams. Through stress and strife and difficulties many and burdens heavy, he brought forward the enterprise to its present large success.

"The great wheels and saws at the mill still sing their song of labor, the massive blocks of marble still come down as yesterday, the blasts on the mountain-side are still heard, the hundreds of men in shop and quarry still toil on, but he who was the moving spirit in all this great enterprise lies cold and still, while those near and dear to him mourn beside the silent

The Number 2 electric B-B flatcar motor was at Marble beside the loading platform, when photographed on September 6, 1941. Poles were mounted on the side of the car to make a framework so a canvas cover could be drawn over the open area between the cabs. The canvas was stored in the box on the car floor. This motor is identified by the large window panes.

PHOTO BY MORRISON A. SMITH,
COLLECTION OF JOHN W. MAXWELL

During the summer of 1942, abandonment proceedings were under way and the wire came down on the electric tramway. The wire was wound onto this drum, mounted on a flat car shown here crossing the Crystal River.

body. He was in truth the 'Father of Marble'.

"A special car, provided for the family by the general manager of the D&RG, left Marble Thursday with his body for Denver. Previously the workmen from the mill and quarry stood in line in the rain for two hours waiting for the funeral procession to start. Carried from the house to a draped carriage, his body was taken to the train by the great team which had so often carried Colonel Meek to and from his home.

"Governor Shafroth of Colorado, who had long been an intimate personal friend of Colonel Meek, requested that the body be allowed to lie in state in Denver in the corridor of the State House from 12 until 2 o'clock Saturday."

"The Marble Booster," dated September 14, 1912, reported on a trolley accident. Four persons met death on the trolley line, including the motorman, the brakeman, a Mexican worker and an eight-year-old Polish girl. The train ran out of control, having lost its straight air brakes, and careened down the line. The motor car made it across the Crystal River bridge, then jumped the track at the loading platform just outside the mill at Marble. The brakeman was crushed under a huge block of marble, the Mexican met instant death when he was thrown off onto the ground and the girl died that evening. The brakeman lost his life when he was thrown against a cliff.

The grades were considered extremely steep for a standard gauge electric line, being 6 to 14-percent. Many news articles list this road as having 17-percent maximum grade. The line was 3-1/2 miles in length. The maximum curvature was 77-degrees, as listed in a monument dealers book.

Before 1915, 20 men would be hired to shovel out drifts or slides on the electric. Shortly thereafter, the "Black Bull" rotary snowplow was built. She had rotary blades at both ends, and entrance for the motorman was gained through the middle of the unit. The rotary would be run up to the quarry during the fall so it would have the advantage of gravity to cut through the three snowslide areas. Along these curves, the road's power lines were taken out each winter.

The winter after the "Black Bull" was built, the company asked "Pop" Sampson to open the road from the quarry. He rounded up the car crew and 12 men with shovels to open up the line. The road was known as "the steepest, slickest, smoothest railroad in the world," as written up in a magazine article. The car crew was very edgy about running the plow because it had never been tried out and no one knew if the brakes would hold.

Everything went well down to the rotary station, where the crew stopped for lunch. The motors were warmed up, the brakes were hot, and the plow was chained to the rail. The crew lunched about an

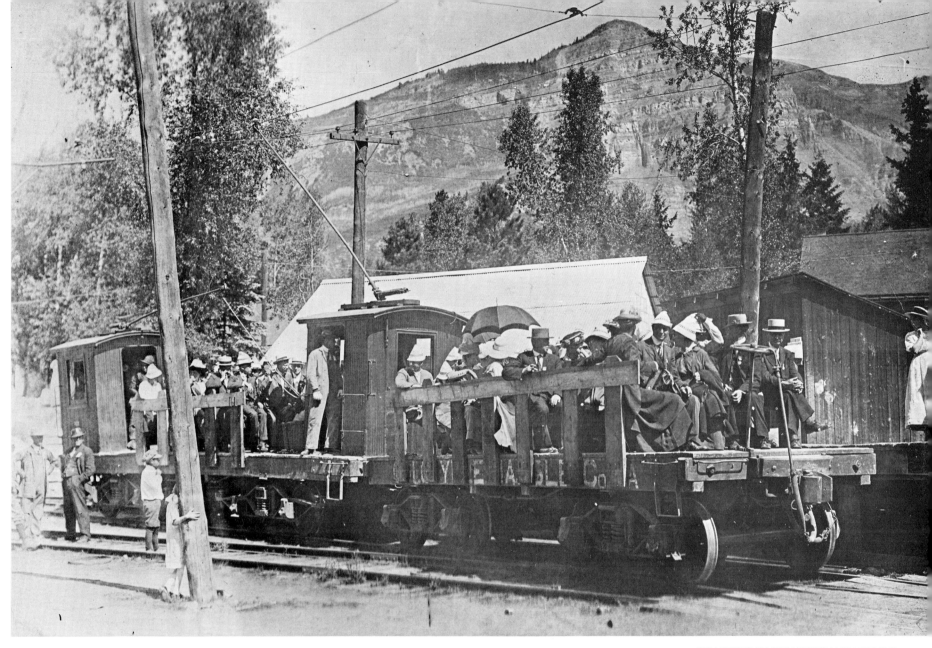

This group of people were Marble Company stockholders -- about to have the thrill of a lifetime riding over the roller-coaster grades of the electric tramway. This was in 1913 at the loading platform of Marble. The Yule Tram is ready to start up the unbelievable 17-percent grade to the quarry. Some of the local children are taking in the sights and sounds created when these strangers from far-away Eastern cities came to town.

hour, just long enough for the wheels to form ice and freeze hard. Elmer Bair started the fan and "Bus" Long unchained the plow and started releasing the air a little at a time until the air was all gone, but there she stood on the brow of the steep hill at the start of the 17-percent drop.

"Bus" next applied one notch of electricity, or juice, as they called it. It just stood there and hummed. Then he gave it two notches, and it still just hummed. He then applied three notches and the plow broke loose -- all at once! Imme-

diately the plow went zooming down the hill at a fast speed. The motorman applied all the brakes and set all the wheels. Pop gave orders to jump and then led the way. One after another they jumped from the careening plow. The snow was soft to land in but the trolley poles made jumping difficult to time a jump so that a pole wouldn't be hit. Elmer Bair was finally the last man left on, having the time of his life watching the others take their comical spills in the snow. Before making his exit, Elmer shut off the fan, and the plow imme-

diately began to slacken off in speed -- much to his relief. The snow piled up in front of the machine bringing it to a stop, because the fan did not suck it on through. The crew ran, or limped, up to find Elmer sitting there with his feet hanging out the door laughing his sides off!

Elmer Bair was one of the motormen on the front end when they hauled the huge marble block down for the tomb of the Unknown Soldier. The second motorcar was hooked on the back to act as an anchor.

PHOTO BY MORRISON A. SMITH, COLLECTION OF JOHN W. MAXWELL

In the last years of operations the electric tram motors were brightly painted in orange, as this photo shows in the fall of 1941. These motors were rebuilt many times due to the derailment of runaway trains on the electric line. Notice that the windows of motor Number 1 were different from the other unit. Originally the motors were painted olive green. The motors had no headlights from the late '30's on.

The electric tram line was still under construction early in 1909 when this photo was taken at Marble. The tramway dropped down to the mill yard after crossing the Crystal River bridge. The bridge used by the steam tractor is still in place and the steam generator plant is yet to be constructed. The marble turntable pit (in front of the enginehouse) is nearly ready for use.

A promotional sale of Corporate bonds by the Colorado Yule Marble Company had brought this group of Eastern capitalists to Marble in 1915. Here they patiently await the highball so they can head up into the high country for the unexpected thrill of a ride over the electric tram to the quarry.

The electric train had just arrived in the mill yard, pulling two flat cars loaded with marble. The workman fixes the hook into the chain of the traveling crane to transport the block of marble.

This view photographed in 1907, shows the finishing mill still under construction and the yard nearly empty of marble. A load had recently arrived from the Yule quarry. The traveling crane had just lifted the block off the flat car and is shown carrying it west to the mill for finishing. Notice the stub-end switch.

The "Black Bull" -- Number 99 --
was an electric rotary snow-plow
built in 1915 for use on the line
between the Yule quarry and the
mill at Marble. The rotary is in
need of paint in this view taken
September 6, 1941. "Spotted"
on its own spur beside the mill
office, the operator would enter
through the doors on the side.
The opposite end had the same
blade setup for backing out of a
drift if necessary.

The Colorado-Yule Marble Co.
Marble, Colorado

Milepost 1 at Forest Lawn made a pleasant scene in 1936 -- with motorman Everett Murphy at the wiggle stick. The only sound other than the forest was the whine of electric motors and the "clickity clack" of wheels on rails. A ride to the quarry took about 20 minutes.

A train of marble is shown here just arriving in Marble in 1912. This may have been a Saturday evening train, carrying quarry-men into town for a night of fun and games. This was the Crystal River bridge, and the steam generator plant can be seen in the background. Notice the old bridge foundation to the right (under the trolley bridge) that was used by the steam tractor.

179

This view was taken on October 11, 1941, shortly before the electric tramway was dismantled by Morse Brothers Machinery of Denver. Arkansas Mountain rises in the background and a glimpse of the Treasury Mountain railroad grade shows above the second trolley pole on the far hillside. This is about one mile out of Marble and was named Forest Lawn.

Smelter Curve, just up from Marble, provided another wreck scene about 1937 when a train ran away downgrade. Hard to control straight air brakes were usually to blame for derailments.

Photographed below Forest Lawn in 1936, the Yule Tram had derailed after running away. This was extremely dangerous because the loaded flats would always run under the motor upon impact. But with any luck, the marble would tumble off before the train came to a smashing halt.

This "Quick-Way Truck Shovel" was shipped into Marble in the late 1930's to clean out rock, mud and snow slides. One trip on the Yule Tram was almost too much for it, as seen here after going over the bank in a derailment.

COLLECTION OF JOHN T. HERMAN

COLLECTION OF MRS. MAURINE BARNES HERMAN

COLLECTION OF JOHN T. HERMAN

This company-financed prospect opening came about in 1909, part way up Yule Creek -- west of Yule Falls -- in quest of slate. Col. Meek soon dropped this venture in favor of putting everything into the marble business.

One of the electric tram motors took off with the birds -- as this wreck of 1910 shows. The motor on the grade below is winching the wreckage up over the bank.

During the winter of 1909, the electric tram line was still laying track and stringing wire. The men are busy fastening the upright that the wire will hang from. The motorman's cab was built off center to allow a walkway into the cab. Some of the ties used on this standard gauge road may have been used ties off some narrow gauge pike.

COLLECTION OF GEORGE T. HARRIS

The "Black Bull" rotary snowplow, Number 99, bites into the fresh snow on the electric line, c. 1936. The snow could be blown out either side (of either end) as the rotary worked downhill with the aid of gravity.

Poised on a curve at a crazy tilt, this electric motor had stopped momentarily one day in 1938 to make line repairs. This photo was taken about one and one-half miles out of Marble.

COLLECTION OF BILL SMITH

The Rotary Station, half-way house on the tramway, was used many times as a lunch stop for the train crew. Ice and food were brought up from Marble by team and wagon. Electric tram motors would stop here to check the brakes before descending the 17-percent grade just beyond. William McManus, standing on the near end of the flat car, was superintendent of the quarry operation in 1909.

184

By October 11, 1941, all that remained of the Booster Station on the electric tram was this phone booth, placed at this spot for emergency calls. Many times trainmen would hike up grade to report a runaway after having "joined the birds". The Booster Station burned at an unknown earlier date.

Photographed near the halfway house in the fall of 1909, this view looks down toward Marble. The grade of the Treasury Mountain Railroad may be seen at the right, above the construction camp tents. Just visible is the switchback on the Treasury Mountain line, swinging over the top of the slide rock area.

This snow slide at Mud Gulch was an annual spring occurance on the electric tram line. A crew of 125 men was called out of the mill to shovel snow up on the road. The snow-shovelers would work the snow up the stair-steps, a job that could last as long as a full week.

Swinging around Windy Point in 1910, the electric tram made a stop for this special photograph. Elk Mountain and Arkansas Mountain rise in the distance, high above Marble. The electric grade curves through a 77-degree curve at this point, swinging back to the north and dropping down the lower hillside.

187

COLLECTION DELL A. MCCOY

About February 1, 1931, the 56-ton block of marble for the Tomb of the Unknown Soldier began moving one mile per day over the electric line to Marble. Elmer Bair was on the lead motor and John Fenton brought up the rear, skidding the block downgrade on two small wheels and an oak timber.

Many of the quarry men who traveled from Marble on the electric tram (to the far right) would arrive at their job on this funicular tram. Looking to the north, the shacks of Quarry Town cling to the hillside in this 1911 photo. This flatcar was operated by cable and fitted with bench seats for passengers. This tram was set up before the railroad was installed and was originally used to lower the blocks of marble to the steam tractor.

The winter of 1908 nearly buried the newly completed Quarry Town -- built high above the road leading up from Marble. The entrances to most of the workers' houses were through ice tunnels. Trips to the outhouses -- perched on the steep hillsides -- could be quite an experience -- and one carelessly placed step could end in catastrophy.

COLLECTION OF MERVIN C. AUDE

COLLECTION OF THE LATE WILLIAM MCMANUS

PHOTO BY GEORGE L. BEAM, COURTESY OF JACKSON THODE

This close-up shows the funicular tram running under the transfer crane along the mainline of the electric tram. Logs were imbedded in the marble walls to support the track here. The houses of Quarry Town are on the ridge above.

WATERCOLOR PAINTING BY DELL A. McCOY

"High Altitude Electric"

A thunder shower rolls over the Yule Creek Valley -- as a train-load of marble leaves the quarry, heading down to Marble. At this high elevation nearly 11,000-feet above sea level - storms form without warning. The Osgood Quarry was near the building to the left, but did not develop into a paying business. The electric motors were painted olive green during the first years of operation and sprouted headlights along with brass whistles.

Yule Creek tumbles past the Yule Quarry loading station in this 1911 view. The most breathtaking operation of the quarry was the lowering of the marble by block-and-tackle onto the waiting tram cars. One mistake could crush a man -- or train -- in a split second. Coal for heating was stored in the bunkers.

As viewed at the end-of-track in the fall of 1941, this late afternoon photo shows the vast amount of second-choice marble dumped out of the quarry diggings.

PHOTO BY MORRISON A. SMITH, COLLECTION OF JOHN W. MAXWELL

COLLECTION OF DELL A. MC COY

The motorman waits patiently for the "High Ball" signal to make the descent from the loading station to the mill at Marble. Fresh-cut blocks of marble are on the flat cars coupled behind the motor car.

By the year 1911, the quarry of the Coloardo Yule Marble Company was in full production. A funicular tram was in use to move stone blocks down the hillside -- while far below, the end-of-track of the electric tram can be seen through the trees. The blacksmith shops and boiler house were in the buildings along the face of the mountain.

PHOTO BY GEORGE L. BEAM, COLLECTION OF JACKSON THODE

PHOTO BY GEORGE L. BEAM, COURTESY OF JACKSON THODE

In 1911 the quarry was cutting out marble blocks faster than the electric tram could haul them down to the mill. Several blocks can be seen on the ground stored with chain around them, ready for the next train. The workmen were hoisted up to the quarry opening in the cage to the left -- which could carry eight to ten people. The stairway had over 300 steps. The transfer crane is down the track where loads were exchanged from the funicular tram, and Quarry Town is just above this.

In this view the photographer was looking west across the Colorado-Yule Marble openings c. 1955. Time and nature have taken their toll of man's wooden structures, but the marble remains almost as pure and white as the day it was left.

PHOTO BY THE LATE JOHN B. SCHUTTE

The quarry was still very much in operation on October 16, 1941, as this workman guides a marble block onto a quarry car. This flatcar would then run about 25-feet to the face of the man-made cliff, where a 50-ton Flory derrick would hoist the block up out of the pit and lower it to the electric tram 110-feet below.

During the last years of operation at the quarry, the workmen went up and down from the end-of-track on the electric tram on this cablecar.

The Ingersoll channeling machine is shown here in 1909, being used to start the work on the Number 3 opening. These machines cost $3,500 and were equipped similar to rock drills. The bits would rise and fall rapidly as the machine moved forward on its track, cutting a groove one-fourth inch wide and 4 to 6-feet deep into the marble floor. The derrick was positioned to lift the blocks out of the quarry and swing them over the tramway below for loading. This derrick had a 50-ton capacity.

In icy silence -- the silence of a tomb -- the stone quarry of the Colorado-Yule Marble Company stood empty and abandoned in July of 1961. Only the drip of water onto the frosty floor could be heard. When the photograph was taken, it was still possible to descend into this huge vault in the heart of the mountain. As of the printing of this book, the wooden steps leading down into the opening had collapsed -- and entrance is virtually impossible.

PHOTO BY MORRISON A. SMITH, COLLECTION OF JOHN W. MAXWELL

It would have been interesting to observe quarrying methods at Colorado-Yule Marble Company's opening Number 3 in 1909. Three channeling machines were in use to open the Number 3 quarry. The workers moved blocks, weighing as much as 50-tons, up and out of this cavernous opening.

In 1930, the Yule-Colorado Company, recently reformed under Jacob Smith, was awarded the contract to furnish marble for the Tomb of the Unknown Soldier. A carefully-quarried block weighing 56-tons was lifted out of the quarry and placed on a home-made railroad car with two low wheels in front and oak timbers left to skid on the rear. The car was then inched down a specially constructed grade -- 200-feet in length -- with a 20-percent grade and 20-degree curve. An additional 600-foot long track connected this with the electric line. Portions of these tracks are visible here photographed on October 11, 1941, looking toward Marble.

This magnificent panoramic photograph of Marble was taken in 1912. The Colorado-Yule Marble Company mill is to the left, with the electric line dropping down the 14-percent grade to the Crystal River bridge. The steam generator plant was the large white building and the enginehouse barn is to the right of this. The Treasury Mountain Railroad grade curves around the barn and heads up the right-of-way to the right. Two boxcars and the Crystal River combination coach Number 2 are spotted on the mainline.

To the right of the coach is a short passing track. The residential section of Marble (shown in the right-hand portion of the photo) was formerly called Clarence, until July 4, 1892, when the two towns merged. Carbonate Creek flows through the land cut just above town. Beaver Lake is to the far right, on the road to Crystal City. The Smelter Bridge crosses the river near the middle of the picture.

TREASURY MOUNTAIN

I n 1896, the Kelly Brothers opened what was known as the Strauss Marble Quarry, built roads and set up a small cutting plant, however, very little business was done. Then the Crystal River Marble Company was incorporated on March 30, 1909, taking over the property of the Strauss Quarry. Their Treasury Mountain Railroad and track was completed August 18, 1910. This was a standard gauge railroad with grades of 4-percent. Two switchbacks were installed at about the halfway point on this track which totaled about 3-1/2 miles in length. Sixty-pound rail was used throughout.

The only engine of this company was a Lima-built Shay, given the Number "1". This geared engine was normally run from Marble to the steam plant at the end-of-track. The engine was housed in a metal shed at the steam plant until it was dismantled in 1948 and scrapped.

Roy Coombs fired the Treasury Mountain Shay to the Strauss Quarry in 1910 for about three weeks, every other day. The trip took about 45-minutes. Two empties were the up-grade limit for the Lima-built locomotive #2052 built 1909.

The Strauss Quarry property was completely idle as of 1915, and then in December of 1928, the Vermont Marble Company formed the Yule-Colorado Marble Company, taking over the Strauss Property. At that time they made a cost survey for rehabilitating the line -- coming up with an estimate of $50,000.00. The project was then dropped.

COLLECTION OF THE LATE WILLIAM MCMANUS

The Treasury Mountain Railroad was under construction in September of 1909 when this scene was photographed. Shay engine Number 1 was pushing flatcar loads of cross ties to the end-of-track. This view was taken in Marble between train movements.

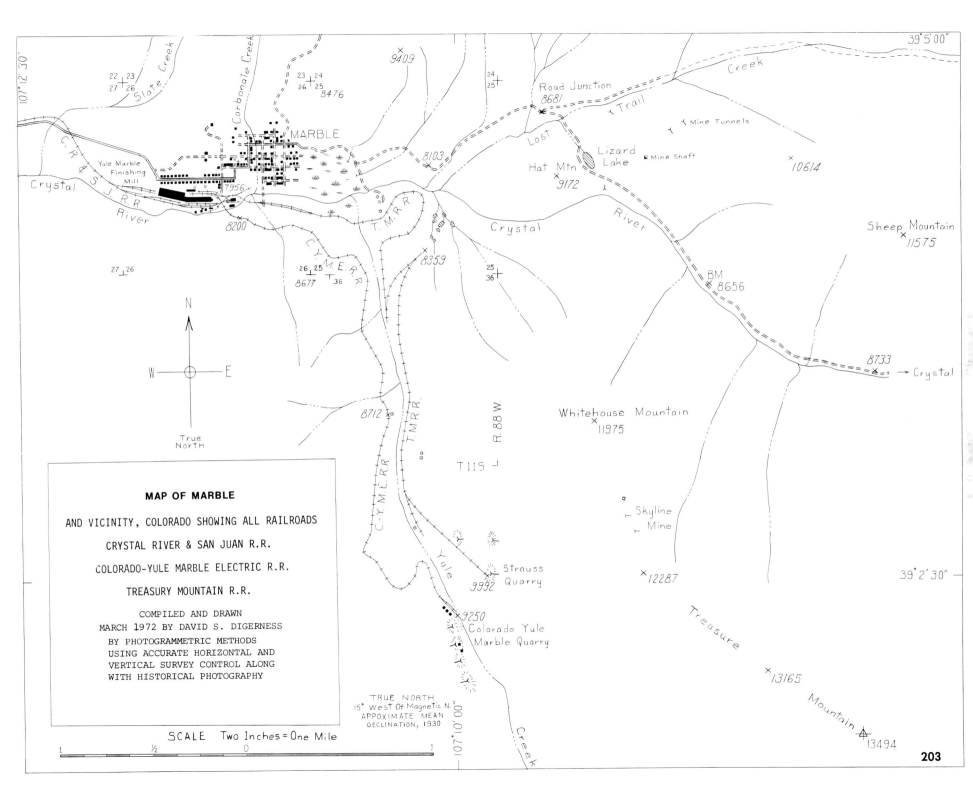

39°5'00"

107°12'30"

9409

22 23
27 26

23 24
26 25
8476

Road Junction
8681

Mine Tunnels

Slate Creek

Carbonate Creek

MARBLE

Yale Marble
Finishing
Mill

C.R.&S.J.R.R.

Crystal

River

8103

8200

7956

Lost

Trail

Lizard
Lake

Mine Shaft

Hat Mtn
9172

×10614

Crystal

River

Sheep Mountain
×11575

T.M.R.R.

C.Y.M.E.R.R.

27 26

26 25
8677 36

8359

25
36

BM
8656

8733 → Crystal

N

W ⊙ E

True
North

8712

T.M.R.R.

C.Y.M.E.R.R.

Whitehouse Mountain
×11975

R.88 W.

T 11 S

Skyline
Mine

×12287

MAP OF MARBLE

AND VICINITY, COLORADO SHOWING ALL RAILROADS

CRYSTAL RIVER & SAN JUAN R.R.

COLORADO-YULE MARBLE ELECTRIC R.R.

TREASURY MOUNTAIN R.R.

COMPILED AND DRAWN
MARCH 1972 BY DAVID S. DIGERNESS
BY PHOTOGRAMMETRIC METHODS
USING ACCURATE HORIZONTAL AND
VERTICAL SURVEY CONTROL ALONG
WITH HISTORICAL PHOTOGRAPHY

Yule

Strauss
Quarry
9992

9250
Colorado Yule
Marble Quarry

Treasure

×13165

Mountain

39°2'30"

TRUE NORTH
15° West Of Magnetic N.
APPOXIMATE MEAN
DECLINATION, 1930

107°10'00"

Creek

SCALE Two Inches = One Mile

1   ½   0   1

⊕13494

Treasury Mountain Railroad Shay geared-engine Number 1 is shown here taking on water for one of its unscheduled trips to the Strauss Quarry run by the Crystal River Marble Company. This view was made in 1910 near the Colorado-Yule Marble Company mill. A finishing mill for the Strauss operation had been planned for construction in Littleton, Colorado; however, nothing ever came of it. Good railroad connections existed in Littleton and there was less chance for damage to shipments of finished marble (as was the case for shipments going out over the CR&SJ).

Someone's home floats by in the Crystal River in this flood scene at Marble, c. 1935. Wreckage from the flood was piling-up at the Treasury Mountain Railroad bridge.

This was the pile trestle leading out of Marble to tap the marble beds of the Crystal River Marble Company. The Treasury Mountain RR. probably started grading in April 1909, and track was completed on August 18, 1910. The mill tailings of the Hoffman & Tischauseer smelter are visible to the left. White House Mountain towers in the distance, with the railroad grade climbing up across the base of the peak into Yule Creek Canyon to the right.

This rare old photo may be of the Lead Bullet Mine, high on the west side of Treasure Mountain c. 1891. High above timberline, only the sure-footed burro was dependable. One by one, the burros are being unloaded of their supply of food and coal. The miner's wash hangs out to air. These men earned every cent they obtained from their mining efforts — and then some.

The Crystal River Marble Company's funicular tramway operated with two incline flatcars. Workers would be loading one at the upper end while the other one was being unloaded at the lower end. The incline flatcars would pass each other half-way up the line. This type of cable car system operates with the assistance of gravity.

PHOTO BY GEORGE L. BEAM, D& RGW COLLECTION COURTESY JACKSON THODE

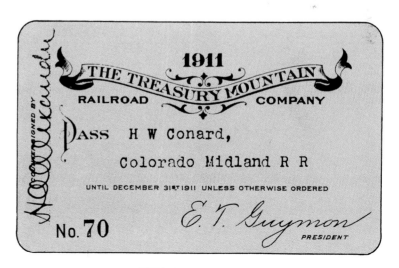

1911
THE TREASURY MOUNTAIN
RAILROAD   COMPANY

Pass   H W Conard,
    Colorado Midland R R

UNTIL DECEMBER 31st 1911 UNLESS OTHERWISE ORDERED

E. T. Guymon
PRESIDENT

No. 70

COUNTERSIGNED BY

The Treasury Mountain's Shay engine Number 1 was stored at the end-of-track from 1915 until it was cut up for scrap in 1948. This photo was probably shot during the depression years of the 1930's. Originally the engine was housed in a metal shed, however, this shed had collapsed by the time this photo was taken.

The powerhouse of the Strauss Quarry still had track running into the big double-doors (on the far right) when this photo was taken in 1935. The road was for wagon travel to the quarry.

Yule Creek cascades past the Treasury Mountain Railroad's Shay as she clears the switchback above Marble. The gondola loaded with marble will be dropped at Marble, picked up by the CR&SJ, dropped at Redstone, picked up by the Crystal River, dropped at Carbondale, picked up by the D&RG and hauled to Littleton, Colorado, for finishing.

"Autumn on the Treasury Mountain"

WATERCOLOR PAINTING BY DELL A. MCCOY

PHOTOS BY GEORGE L. BEAM, D&RGW COLLECTION COURTESY OF JACKSON THODE

The cable funicular tram line connecting the Strauss Quarry of the Crystal River Marble Company with the Treasury Mountain RR. is shown in this scene. An upright crane was located at the bottom of the cable line. This would lift blocks of marble into waiting gondolas spotted on the siding. The electric tram grade crosses the valley near the top with the half-way house on the sharp curve to the right. This view was photographed in 1911 by a D&RG railroad photographer. He was looking toward the west, across the Yule Creek drainage basin.

The Strauss Quarry was in production when this photo was taken in 1911 by the D&RG photographer. The quarry was off to a good start, but ran out of funds due to the lack of sales and the high cost of building the Treasury Mountain Railroad. This is one of several openings and this upright crane loaded the funicular flat car.

211

Inside the main quarry of the Crystal River Marble Company, most of the implements of the industry still remained in 1971, just as they were left 56 years before (in 1915). Far enough away from civilization, the Strauss quarry has remained almost as it was through the years.

This opening of the Crystal River Marble Company -- known as the Strauss Quarry -- was the largest one of several. The size of the opening may be judged by the hikers entering it in 1971. A hoist drum is in the foreground.

In this 1971 view (to the right) dumped marble, light iron rail and rotted ties combine to show the remains of an unfulfilled company dream. If architects had been properly trained to incorporate native stone in planning buildings, this dream would have come true. But because of the basic lack of knowledge and appreciation of the fine arts on the part of Americans, these great deposits of beautiful stone will remain untouched.

A hoist drum was still near its original position in this photo of the Strauss Quarry taken during the fall of 1971. This hoist shown at the lower right, probably ran the cable on the upright crane for lifting blocks of marble.

PHOTOS THIS PAGE BY RONALD F. RUHOFF

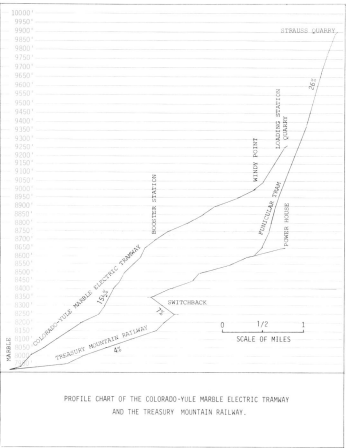

PROFILE CHART OF THE COLORADO-YULE MARBLE ELECTRIC TRAMWAY
AND THE TREASURY MOUNTAIN RAILWAY.

PHOTO BY DELL A. MCCOY

Located approximately one-third of the distance between Marble and Crystal City, Lizard Lake provides a colorful interlude along the way. Between the two villages the road is narrow, steep and twisting -- not to mention the ruts and rocks encountered in the road's surface. This stops all but the bravest of flatland tourists -- who dauntlessly push their automobiles over this wildly beautiful stretch of back-country mountain road, swallowing hard to overcome their fear of heights!

In 1958, the compressor house of the Wild Horse Mill still held a charm all its own. Probably built in 1890, this structure proves once again that a wise person will build on a solid foundation. The Crystal River falls through the rocks at the edge of Crystal City (hidden in the trees).

RONALD F. RUHOFF

Engineers in camp.

Looking down on Crystal City in 1890, it is evident the settlement was a booming mining camp. The headwaters of the Crystal River begin at Schofield Park, located a few miles behind Crystal Peak in the distance. The North Fork of the Crystal River is to the left.

JOHN SMITH COLLECTION, CAMP AND PLANT

The Devils Punch Bowl along the Crystal River has been the site of several fatal automobile accidents involving Eastern tourists visiting the area. The road is so steep at this point that persons inexperienced in mountain driving can easily lose control, either going up or down grade. A vehicle may slide, even though the brakes are locked, due to the loose gravel and rocks found on this road. Photographed in 1967.

PHOTO BY DELL A. McCOY

Railroad Equipment Rosters

CRYSTAL RIVER RAILWAY

LOCOMOTIVE NUMBER	BUILDER AND NUMBER	DATE BUILT	TYPE	GAUGE	CYLINDERS	DRIVERS	WEIGHT ON DRIVERS	DATE SCRAPPED	TENDER
11	Baldwin, 13634	1893	0-8-0	3'-0"	17 x 20"	38"	82,000	(?)	Slope Back
1	Baldwin, 13176	1893	2-8-0	4'-8½"	20 x 24"	45"	156,400	1920	Sq. Tank

CRYSTAL RIVER RAILROAD

LOCOMOTIVE NUMBER	BUILDER AND NUMBER	DATE BUILT	TYPE	GAUGE	CYLINDERS	DRIVERS	WEIGHT ON DRIVERS	DATE SCRAPPED	TENDER
1	Baldwin, 18092	1900	2-8-0	4'-8½"	22 x 28"	50"	170,000	1940's	Sq. Tank
101	Baldwin, 17872	1900	2-8-0	3'-0"	17 x 20"	38"	82,000	1950	Slope Back
102	Baldwin, 17717	1900	2-8-0	3'-0"	17 x 20"	38"	82,000	1951	Slope Back
103	Baldwin, 21757	1903	2-8-0	3'-0"	18 x 20"	38"	103,000	1949	Sq. Tank
103	R.I. Loco Works	(?)	4-4-0	4'-8½"	18 x 26"	55"	106,000	(?)	Sq. Tank
701	Baldwin, 10503	1889	4-6-0	4'-8½"	18 x 24"	55"	109,000	(?)	Sq. Tank

CRYSTAL RIVER & SAN JUAN RAILWAY

LOCOMOTIVE NUMBER	BUILDER AND NUMBER	DATE BUILT	TYPE	GAUGE	CYLINDERS	DRIVERS	WEIGHT ON DRIVERS	DATE SCRAPPED	TENDER
6	Unknown	1906	2-6-0	4'-8½"				1915	Sq. Tank

CRYSTAL RIVER & SAN JUAN RAILROAD

LOCOMOTIVE NUMBER	BUILDER AND NUMBER	DATE BUILT	TYPE	GAUGE	CYLINDERS	DRIVERS	WEIGHT ON DRIVERS	DATE SCRAPPED	TENDER
1	Baldwin, 11717	1891	4-6-0	4'-8½"	18 x 24"	55"	109,000	1944-'47	Sq. Tank
2	Baldwin, 20459	1902	2-6-0	4'-8½"	18 x 24"	51"	100,000	1943	Sq. Tank
3	Baldwin, 29826	1906	2-6-0	4'-8½"	18 x 24"	51"	100,000	1942	Sq. Tank

COLORADO-YULE MARBLE ELECTRIC TRAMWAY

MOTOR NUMBER	DATE PURCH.	TYPE	GAUGE	DISPOSITION
100 Renumbered 1	1910	B+B	4'-8½"	Scrapped at Morse Bros. Machinery, Denver
101 Renumbered 2	1910	B+B	4'-8½"	Scrapped at Morse Bros. Machinery, Denver
99	1915	Double-Ended Rotary Snowplow	4'-8½"	Scrapped at Morse Bros. Machinery, Denver

TREASURY MOUNTAIN RAILROAD

LOCO. NO.	BUILDER	DATE PURCH.	TYPE	GAUGE	DRIVERS	SCRAPPED
1	Blt. Lima No. 2052	1909	0-4-4-0TG	4'-8½"	28"	1948

LOCOMOTIVE NOTES

The Crystal River Railway's first locomotive was a narrow gauge 0-8-0, No. 11. This engine was returned to Baldwin in 1894 and rebuilt as a 2-8-0. It was sold to the Central of Georgia's narrow gauge Greenville branch, was standard-gauged in 1907 and given the number, 804. In either 1904 or 1907 the engine was sold to the Gainsville Midland. SI&E then purchased it, item No. 973, and in 1915 sold it to the Mt. Airy & Eastern as their No. 9. It was returned to SI&E, item No. 1088, and once again sold—this time to the Compania Azucarera Madrazo of Cuba in November of 1916. This firm designated the engine No. 3.

The second locomotive owned by the Crystal River Railway was a standard gauge 2-8-0, No. 1. This engine was sold to the Colorado & Wyoming in 1901 and designated No. 201.

The first engine owned by the Crystal River Railroad was a husky 2-8-0, No. 1, known as "Bull of the Woods." This engine was also sold to the Colorado & Wyoming where she became No. 7 in 1906. Narrow gauge 2-8-0's Nos. 101, 102 and 103 became the D&RG's 430, 431 and 432 in 1916. These engines were later renumbered 360, 361 and 375 during the D&RG's renumbering program of 1923 and 1924.

C&W No. 103 was leased for service on the standard gauge from 1906 through 1910. She then returned to the C&W. This engine is believed to have come from the Union Pacific Railroad. No. 701 was leased for service on the standard gauge from January 1, 1911, until late in 1912, and made trips from Carbondale to Marble and return under some unknown arrangement. She was then sent back to the C&W for several years of service on that line.

The CR&SJ's No. 6 may have been purchased from the Union Pacific also; however, no records exist to verify this belief.

CR&SJ No. 1 was purchased in 1915 from the D&RG (their No. 532). No. 2 was bought in 1930 from the Clarendon & Pittsford (their No. 5), while No. 3 came from the C&P in 1936 (their No. 6). Both No. 2 and No. 3 were 0-6-0's with slope-back tenders, and were converted by the CR&SJ to 2-6-0's with square-back tenders.

Wheel sizes were changed to a larger diameter on Yule Tram motors 100 and 101 about 1912 to fit larger brake shoes. Reportedly this caused technical problems, resulting in run-aways, such as the one which caused the death of Col. Meek and the tragic derailment shortly thereafter. Straight air braking was in use and could have contributed to the trouble.

TMR No. 1 ran over the CR&SJ for about three weeks in 1912 while the CR&SJ's No. 6 was being re-flued. During that same period No. 1 also ran trips up to the Strauss quarry for loads. She was eventually cut up for scrap at the end-of-track near the quarry and her crown sheet may be seen resting near the CR&SJ's former end-of-track at Marble.

The assortment of graphic railroadianna on the following page was gathered from contributors on the East Coast and in Colorado for this valuable display of history.

MORRIS W. ABBOTT -- BRAIN BADGE AND ELK MOUNTAIN COUPON
MICHAEL KOCH -- ELK MOUNTAIN STOCK CERTIFICATE AND COUPON
JACKSON THODE -- CRYSTAL RIVER AND CR&SJ PASSES
CHARLES RYLAND -- TREASURY MOUNTAIN AND CR&SJ PASSES
BILL SMITH -- D&RGW TRIP PASS TO MARBLE
WESTERN COLLECTION, DENVER PUBLIC LIBRARY -- ASPEN & WESTERN PASS
RONALD SCHILP -- CR&SJ TICKET
DELL A. MCCOY -- SPIKE COLLECTION

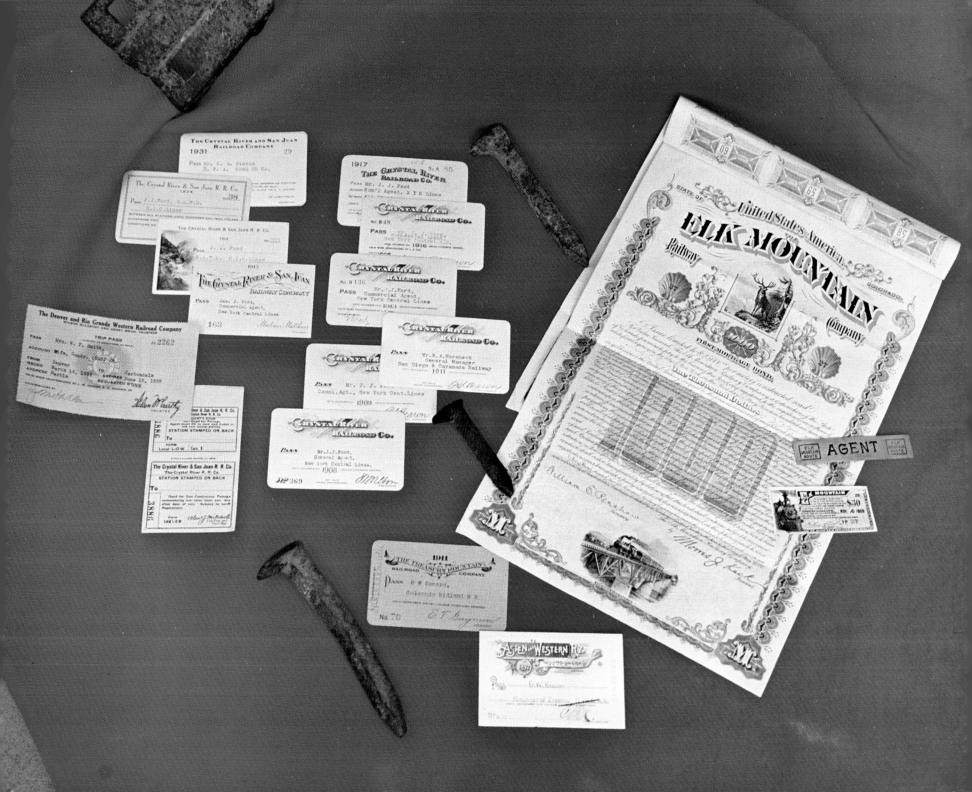

INDEX

* Asterisk indicates text material

CRYSTAL RIVER RAILROAD

CAR EQUIPMENT ROSTER — C. 1903

TYPE EQUIPMENT	GAUGE	TOTAL NUMBERS	NUMBER	LENGTH	WIDTH	HEIGHT	CAPACITY	WEIGHT
Combination Coach	4'-8½''	1	1	40'-0''	9'-0''	14'-0''	Seating 28	34,500
Flanger	4'-8½''	1	A	21'-1½''	4'-4''	12'-0''	----------	34,000
Derrick	4'-8½''	1	A1	30'-0''	8'-0''	13'-10''	----------	38,000
Snowplow	4'-8½''	1	AB2	38'-3''	6'-6''	14'-3''	----------	141,000
Way Car	3'-0''	2	01 02	26'-5½''	6'-9½''	14'-8''	----------	19,000
Flanger	3'-0''	1	B1	18'-0''	3'-6''	11'-6''	----------	28,100
Box Car	3'-0''	1	101	31'-5½''	6'-9½''	11'-6''	50,000	20,000
Flat Car	3'-0''	3	1-3	32'-0''	7'-4''	5'-6''	50,000	16,400
Ingoldsby Dump Cars	3'-0''	40	201-240	35'-1''	7'-8''	7'-2''	50,000	23,500

NOTE: The baggage compartment of Combination Coach No. 2 measured 7'-9'' in length. Rotary Snowplow No. AB2 had an extra set of narrow gauge (3'-0'') trucks, allowing it to be used on both standard gauge and narrow gauge trackage.

In Appreciation

The Crystal River Pictorial was developed over a period of eleven years. The name, "Crystal River & San Juan," was enough inspiration to begin a search for information which led -- in final form -- to this printed book.

Many of the facts included in the book came from first-hand interviews held with people that lived and worked in the Crystal River district of Colorado. William McManus -- for example -- went to work for the Crystal River & San Juan Railroad shortly after its start. He and his wife related many heart-warming experiences of that day. These fine people passed away recently, leaving their treasured collection of photographs and other memorabilia to their children, Mr. and Mrs. John McManus. The children then allowed Sundance Limited the exclusive privilege of diligently searching through this excellent collection of historic Crystal River Valley material. Beyond this, Mr. and Mrs. McManus allowed the publishers to copy directly from each photo, which made it possible to produce the sharp detail afforded in each picture.

Another dear friend, Charles Orlosky of Marble, also died before completion of this book. He and Mrs. Orlosky searched out very rare photos for the publishers and related their experiences about the town of Marble. Without their knowledge, the mill workings and shop interiors would have remained a mystery. Another real friend, Roy Coombs, as a child personally knew J. C. Osgood and advanced through the years working on the railroads of the valley. Through his experiences, many early facts came to light.

Deepest appreciation is extended to Fred and Jo Muzzulla for their personal interest in getting this book off to a start through the use of several rare photos from their collection.

One of the finest gentlemen to assist the publishers in the gathering of photographs and information has been Jackson Thode of the Denver & Rio Grande Western Railroad. His collection provided answers to many mysteries about the earliest railroading in the Crystal River Valley.

Special thanks goes to Robert LeMassena for the use of his valuable collection of Crystal River district photographs, passes and historical information which appear in various parts of this book. Unearthed through his extensive correspondence with friends and acquaintances from all over the country, this material has been of utmost importance.

John W. Maxwell provided special service by loaning several valuable photographs from his collection for use in this book. And Richard Kindig opened his treasure file of photos for use here. David S. Digerness went to great lengths to search through his collection for photos and maps.

The Rev. Morris Chafky donated the use of the very rare conductor's booklet. Special thanks goes to Mrs. Maurine Barnes Herman for her collection of photos. Robert Richardson of the Colorado Railroad Museum also did extensive work toward this book. John T. Herman and his wife are especially remembered for their photos and those of their many friends. Charles Garland also brought to light many unknown facts about the marble quarries. C. F. & I. -- along with their subsidiary, the Colorado & Wyoming Railroad -- furnished an untold amount of facts from their vaults for use in this book. Mid-Continent Coal & Coke Company deserves recognition for allowing the publishers the use of maps of the railroad right-of-way. Bill Smith related his facts as one of the last engineers on the road. George and Dorothy White, along with their daughter, Pat Zollinger, took special efforts to assist in providing material for this book. Mr. and Mrs. Ernest Gerbaz of Glenwood Springs had a great deal to do with the formative years on this work, by introducing their exclusive collection for the author's use.

A very special "thanks" is also extended to the following people who furnished so much toward this work of art, as well as to many others who remain un-named:

MORRIS W. ABBOTT,
MERVIN C. AUDE,
COLORADO RAILROAD MUSEUM,
ELMOR FREDERICK,
DEL GERBAZ,
CHARLES GERTIG FAMILY,
ED HALEY,
MRS. CLAUD HALL,
ROME AND RUBY ISLER,
MICHAEL KOCH,
MR. AND MRS. REES,
FRANCIS RIZZARI,
JOHN ROBINSON,
RICHARD RONZIO,
RONALD F. RUHOFF,
CHARLES RYLAND,
ESTHER SANCHEZ,
RONALD SCHILP,
MARY SCHUTTE,
LEN SHOEMAKER,
U. S. FOREST SERVICE,
U. S. GEOLOGICAL SURVEY LIBRARY,
DUANE VANDENBUSCHE,
TRUMAN YOUNG
VERMONT MARBLE COMPANY and the
DENVER PUBLIC LIBRARY,
    WESTERN HISTORY DEPT.

A Fond Farewell . . .

PHOTO BY S. L. LOGUE, COLLECTION EVERETTE L. DEGOLYER, JR.

During the fall of 1946, engines Number 1 and 2 of the Crystal River & San Juan Railroad rust away on a Carbondale side track before being hauled out for scrapping. Strangely enough, these locomotives sat on the wye in Carbondale for approximately four years awaiting disposition. These engines, along with Number 3, were the last to operate along the Crystal River.

The Crystal River Railroad herald reproduced on the back cover and title page was drawn from the emblematic lettering on the engine cab of the "Bull of the Woods". The columbine flowers are the official Colorado State flower. J. C. Osgood lovingly named his railroad "The Columbine Route" because of their presence in the Crystal River Valley.